TURNING MANNERS INTO MONEY

Start Your Journey to Success

ROBIN MARRIOTT

I met Robin several years ago through business connections and was instantly impressed with her professional style and passion for speaking and coaching. Robin is gifted in creating a personalized strategy utilizing updated etiquette to motivate CEOs, physicians, business owners, staff, and different organizations with specific techniques that allow for increased ROI and peaceful working conditions. Robin's presentations are energetic and interactive, engaging her audience with relevant, timely information. Get ready to smile, laugh, and learn techniques that could benefit you in a business environment or your next social event.

~ Lisa H. Harrington, CEO – Abiding Strategy®

In this book, Robin reminds and provides updated information on what it takes to make great first impressions, engage clients and patients, and truly win people over with simple, personalized techniques for businesses to be successful. Every business owner, executive, and employee should read this and implement her advice!

~ Judy Gamin, CEO Executive Medicine of Texas, Speaker, and Best-Selling Author

Publisher Information

Robin Marriott

401 N Carroll Ave. Suite 107

Southlake, TX 76092

For more information visit mannersmeanmoney.com or contact robin@mannersmeanmoney.com

ISBN 979-8-9871079-2-8 (softcover)

ISBN 979-8-9871079-3-5 (ebook)

Cover design: Terry Dugan

Background image: Michal@AdobeStock

Handshake graphic: PictureXpress@AdobeStock

Editing: Cristina Wright

Proofreading: Vickie Deppe

Interior design: Ben Wolf, Inc.

Publishing services provided by BelieversBookServices.com

First printing: 2024

Printed in the United States of America

CONTENTS

PREFACE

In the early 2000s, it became obvious that executives, providers, businesses, and individuals could all benefit in many ways by practicing good manners. Most people don't realize the correlation between the subconscious effect of reducing unspoken fear and creating a relatable atmosphere with people of all levels by being educated and updated in modern manners, especially in this post-pandemic society. After teaching and writing personalized curricula for businesses, executives, medical providers, civic groups, and individuals, utilizing my degrees, certifications, and firsthand knowledge in correlating occupations, I have created a unique three-step acronym to help you remember basic rules of manners (this isn't an exhaustive etiquette book, but a practical application) to earn client trust and respect, create positive office morale, and ultimately increase your ROI and financial goals. Take time to read and learn about this three-step acronym, real-life examples, and practical tips to start your journey to success. Remember, it pays to mind your manners.

FOREWORD

Few Americans—past, present, or future—have taken such "deep dives" into so many professions as Robin Marriott. Not only has she achieved excellence in all of them, but—sometimes with pad in hand and always with mind engaged—she has discovered critical elements that run like skeins of thread in the fabric of our lives. All people, whatever their lot and wherever they serve, crave validation, fairness, and kind treatment.

The "speed of locomotion" whirling all around us causes regard for these elements to grow dim, if not disappear completely. In truth, much of what has been lost as we strive to co-exist with one another may be traced back to the Golden Rule. We yearn to be treated in the manner we think we're treating others! An expression attributed to a venerable public servant from Texas, the late Sam Rayburn (a Texan who served as Speaker of the United States House of Representatives), now seems foreign to our culture. It was he who claimed we must "go along to get along."

There are many reasons suggesting that for our society to get along, much more intentionality must be employed. And that's where Robin comes in. Armed with an undergraduate degree in business and a master's degree in secondary and higher education, she has a common-sense approach to success, causing her expertise to be sought by numerous leading professionals. Much of that common sense comes into focus under the general heading of manners, or by its more formal name of yesteryear, etiquette.

Reflecting on the roads she has trod, Robin has developed creative ways to earn clients' trust, create positive office morale, make strong first impressions, and improve both internal and external communication. Not only are these topics worthy of ongoing emphasis, but they'll also lead to more profitability when applied.

She has written and personalized such material for numerous companies and medical practices over the years and has been the keynote speaker for many conferences and workshops. Her dynamism—both in print and on the platform—evokes the same comments heard at her speaking engagements: "It's great to see you again!"

In her new book, *Turning Manners into Money*, Robin's sincerity and commitment to the common good are evident. She is trustworthy and respected, careful always to be associated with what is positive. She reads, observes, and assists along life's way. Also central to her life are a thirty-seven-year marriage to her minister husband, Dr. Ronny Marriott, and her three grown children. She endears herself to others with a quick and memorable smile. Robin admits to favoring several authors, including the inimitable Dr. Theodor Seuss Geisel, a children's book author best known as Dr. Seuss. One of his poems is titled, "My Uncle Terwilliger on the Art of Eating Popovers." He recited it in 1977 when he received an honorary degree from Lake Forest College. Its lesson about the critical need for believability is central to Robin Marriott's life.

My uncle ordered popovers
from the restaurant's bill of fare.
And, when they were served,
he regarded them with a penetrating stare.

Then he spoke great Words of Wisdom
as he sat there on that chair:
"To eat these things," said my uncle,
"You must exercise great care.

You may swallow down what's solid
BUT
you must spit out the air!"

And as you partake of the world's bill of fare,
that's darned good advice to follow.
Do a lot of spitting out the hot air.
And be careful what you swallow.

Dr. Seuss loved to write but hated to speak. On this occasion, the audience at graduation offered a standing ovation to hear such great truth in what may have been the shortest commencement speech ever!

Dr. Don Newbury
Chancellor, Howard Payne University

*A student once asked Peter Drucker to
tell him the most important thing in business.
After a pause, Drucker said,
"Good manners."*[1]

Chapter One

TURNING MANNER$ INTO MONEY

Bill, a new attorney in town, needed to find a bank he could use for his law practice. Knowing he would be developing a close relationship with the chosen bank, he wanted one that would be professional, easy to work with, reliable, and impressive to future clients. While setting up his new office, Bill decided to call one of the potential banks on his list and set up an appointment with the manager. He was a little taken aback by his experience on the call. After working his way through the phone tree several times, he finally was able to speak with a live person. The bank employee who answered sounded cold and annoyed. Bill proceeded by introducing himself as a new attorney who had just moved to town and wanted to speak with the manager. The employee quickly replied in a huffy tone that he would have to come into the bank because she couldn't help him over the phone. Knowing time was of the essence in getting his affairs in order, Bill reluctantly decided to drive to the bank to see if he could meet the manager and make a decision as to where he would be doing business.

It was a hot Texas summer day as Bill pulled into the parking lot after battling heavy traffic. He just wanted to find a shady spot to park his car and make a mad dash into the air-conditioned building. Bill had worked in some prestigious law firms with high-dollar clients and understood the importance of selecting businesses that would help set the stage when entertaining clients of differing financial levels.

Upon approaching the front door of the bank, Bill couldn't help but notice the overflowing trash can with a syrupy substance running down the side of the receptacle. Was the cleaning crew running behind that day? He opened the door to escape the heat and was expecting to smell fine leather that one would normally experience in a place like this; but instead, he noticed a strong odor and a sweaty carnival setting came to mind. (Unbeknownst to him, the cleaning crew had changed products to save money and used a cheap one with an overbearing odor.) "That's okay," thought Bill. He must have come in at the wrong moment; it would pass. He stood in the doorway for a few minutes, obviously new to the place, examining the lobby for directions on where to proceed to find the bank manager.

Bill, dressed in his tailor-made suit with monogrammed cuffs, starched shirt with pocket square, and expensive designer shoes commanded attention as he walked through the door; he was obviously a successful businessman ready to do business. He caught the eye of a few bank employees behind a counter when he entered; one was scrolling on her phone, and the other two were engaged in a lighthearted conversation. Bill cleared his throat a couple of times, thinking someone would greet him. Finally, he had to approach the counter and ask if he could speak to the bank manager. The two employees who were engaged in conversation looked up while the third person continued to scroll on her phone. Bill asked again about seeing the bank manager, but the employees looked at each other and continued their conversation—someone had a new boyfriend. Bill, feeling a little frustrated, once again asked for the manager and much to his surprise was told to have a seat and someone would take care of it. Despite being unimpressed, Bill decided to meet the manager and see if the bank would be a good fit for his many high-dollar trans-actions.

Bill understood the importance of putting one's best foot forward to woo clients and conduct business with all types of professionals, regardless of their different educational and financial levels. A savvy and classy business professional, Bill knew to shop around before conducting business, but so far, his shopping experience wasn't going as he had hoped. He stood behind one of the leather couches in the lobby as he waited for the manager and examined everything. The coffee pot in the corner of the lobby had long since been emptied, and there was a slight aroma of burned coffee that could be detected after the overwhelming smell of cheap cleaner had dissipated. Two large ferns in clay pots were badly in need of water. Several outdated magazines and dirty paper cups were scattered on a worn coffee table.

Finally, the bank manager appeared. Bill couldn't help but notice the manager's wrinkled pants that were two inches too short, a dress shirt that was a size too small with bulging buttons, and what appeared to be a spaghetti stain. Bill immediately extended his hand for an introduction, and as the manager opened his mouth to speak, it became apparent that perhaps a breath mint might be called for. Bill and the manager spoke for a few minutes, and the manager offered some great financial incentives for Bill's business, but Bill was still in shopping mode. They finished their conversation and Bill turned to leave saying, "I'll be in touch." As he grabbed the door handle, he heard the bank manager shout across the lobby, "Make sure you fill out an online survey about your great experience here today." Bill knew immediately he wouldn't be filling out the survey or giving his business to that bank. He went down the street to check out the next bank on his list.

Can you relate to a scenario like this? Have you looked forward to doing business with a certain place or making new friends to only be turned off by appearance, odor, demeanor, and callous interpersonal skills? The skill and finesse of dealing with people is an art. In a post-pandemic society, there are certain skills everyone could be reminded of.

Your Brain and Manners

The amygdala is a small almond-shaped structure inside your brain. It detects danger and plays a part in emotional control and learning. Fear is the main emotion the amygdala controls, and it carries information from your senses, especially smell (which is why scents can connect strongly to emotions). Your amygdala also connects to brain areas that process vision and hearing. This book will touch on some of these other senses, and it will become evident how the amygdala can affect people positively to reduce fear and create pleasant experiences.[1]

By using courtesy, you are creating a non-threatening environment for whomever you are interacting with. If you can make people feel comfortable, you can earn their trust, gain new clients or patients, keep warm friendships, and boost office morale, even if your audience hasn't been trained in proper manners. After all, manners are about showing respect for others and being cognizant of their needs. When you calm their subconscious fears, you create trust and rapport. This isn't a medical book or an exhaustive book on manners but an easy-to-remember method and awareness of etiquette to keep you on track and learn how to utilize your manners. Perhaps you can turn them into money.

Whether you are making new friends, securing new clients, impressing a boss, getting along with co-workers, or just trying to make more money, creating and perfecting your presence (and consequently, widening your sphere of influence) may be the key. There are many self-help books available to teach you how to do all of these things, but one of the easiest methods is to know, understand, and employ the principles of etiquette so you can get along with different personality types and gain respect. People like to do business and make relationships with others they can trust, relate to, and feel comfortable with. There is an art to making people feel comfortable, and good manners, if used properly, can do just that. Rules of etiquette have changed throughout the years, so brushing up on new techniques and learning existing ones can be helpful in business or life in general.

People worldwide have been isolated and become comfortable with the status quo; personal desires and comforts have become prominent with courtesies quickly disappearing. Much like a butterfly emerges from a cocoon, people are back out in public and may need to break free from old habits and routines and take a refresher course to make new friends, secure new clients, impress a boss, or be reminded of some basics to get along with others.

Have you been to the grocery store, theater, ballpark, or other places post-pandemic and noticed the difference in attitude, politeness, customer service, and common courtesy? Just as a baker goes to a recipe book (well maybe the internet these days) to find the ingredients and directions to make an appetizing dessert, it is well to know the ingredients to become a desirable, attractive business owner, employee, or good friend. After all, you can't make the recipe if you don't know the ingredients and directions to be successful in your cooking endeavor. Just think, if everyone knew how to mix in the perfect amount of ingredients, we could all enjoy the sweet benefits of a positive work environment, healthy friendships, courteous shoppers, and, ultimately, an increase in financial success and reputation. Consider this your cookbook to be reminded of the ingredients that go into a great recipe. In this case, you are the baker, utilizing the ingredients even if others don't know what they are, to mix a tasty recipe for success so people will be pleased with what you have to offer and want to come back for more.

We live in an ever-changing world with people traveling and moving to new areas, different generations with varying ideas, and new businesses emerging every day. Let's face it, some people get on our nerves and are hard to deal with and some have become accustomed to their isolated lives and need a few reminders. Utilizing and disseminating simple social skills allows people to have a basic knowledge and understanding of how to relate to each other across multiple generations. This helps eliminate awkwardness and annoyance. Like a recipe that explains how to combine the proper ingredients in the right order, this book highlights etiquette rules so everyone can enjoy the benefits of a happier work environment, earn the respect and trust of clients, create happier relationships, and earn more money in business deals.

Discerning What Works

We all come from different backgrounds and cultures, so discernment is vital when utilizing these ideas. But the main idea is to make people feel comfortable. If you aren't skilled in discernment, you may need to engage a friend or co-worker to help you read a situation to better yourself. What works for one person may not work for another, so knowing the basic idea of etiquette, learning to pivot when necessary, and utilizing discernment skills are important when practicing these ideas. Let me say that again, learning to discern or read a person is key.

There are many etiquette methods and strategies to remember to create great business and personal relationships, but I have a simple acronym to utilize in different situations to remind yourself and stay on point. What is the acronym? I'm glad you asked! Instead of melting under intense heat, remember the acronym of ICE: Impressions, Communication, and Empathy.

The ice we use every day comes in different shapes and sizes and is used for many different things. Some ice gets frosty, while some is clear. Ice is used for medical purposes, as well as packing, healing, cooking, and drinking. One of the most common uses of ice is for ice cream. After the perfect recipe has been mixed, the sweet cream must be placed in a cylinder packed with ice, and churned with a hand crank (like in the days of old) or by an electric ice cream maker. There isn't anything better than enjoying an ice cream on a hot summer day, and isn't it amazing how it seems to soothe even the most savage beast? Another popular use for ice is in sports after a player experiences an injury. Ice packs, ice baths, and other icy products are used to help with an injury.

Just like the everyday ice we use, incorporating the principles of ICE in different situations can be very beneficial by remembering Impression, Communication, and Empathy.

The details of this three-step acronym are presented on the following pages. Use this method in your next interaction, and perhaps you won't feel yourself melting under pressure but skating to success and even becoming more profitable.

- Benjamin Franklin

Utilize this three-step ICE method which we will explore with quotes, real life examples, and practical tips. Use Benjamin Franklin's advice by learning how to improve your manners along with the Impressions you are subconsciously or consciously making, the Communication styles you are using, and the Empathy you share.

The format is easy to follow:

I - IMPRESSIONS
C – COMMUNICATION
E - EMPATHY

Let's get started turning your manners into money!

Chapter Two

IMPRESSIONS

TURN MANNERS INTO MONEY WHILE BREAKING THE ICE

FROZEN IN TIME

First impressions are vital in meeting a new client, friend, or boss. According to Forbes Magazine, you have seven seconds to make a first impression, so use it wisely! [1]

Think about the last person you met and your initial impression. Did they intrigue you to start or continue a conversation? What kind of vibe did you pick up on? According to Will Rogers, "You never get a second chance to make a first impression."

NAVIGATING THE GLACIERS

Many years ago, I was working in a large organization in a department that dealt with creating positive first impressions, organizing seminars to teach employees how to better themselves and the organization, orchestrating wow experiences for new clients, and promoting a positive all-around environment. We studied lengthy data and proven strategies that help with customer satisfaction, taught employees these strategies, and modeled them to inspire and encourage everyone, raising the level of excellence. Our department was doing well, and our method was so widely accepted that we came to a point where we needed more staff to help facilitate and disseminate our best-foot-forward message. We studied some of the most successful companies known for making clients feel welcome and satisfied, and we adapted those strategies in our organization. When working in a career where you are paid to notice details and promote excellence, it becomes extremely difficult to "unsee" sloppy performances or presentations.

Since our department was growing, we needed another team member to help educate our organization about the idea of going above and beyond. The call went out, and we started taking applications for the perfect fit for our department. Being trained and entrenched in the subject of first impressions, we had high standards for the position. I've been the interviewer and interviewee many times, so I had a pretty good idea of what to expect, but this one proved to be rather interesting. Three of us had the task of adding to our team, and after pouring over resumes, it was time to meet in person. We assembled in the conference room and invited our first applicant to enter. In walked a middle-aged lady dressed in a conservative but slightly tight mini skirt, baggy jacket, and half-tucked blouse with her arms full of colored folders and an oversized, worn leather handbag draped across one shoulder. I immediately thought she must not have noticed her wild, windblown hair in the mirrored elevator ride up to the eighth floor.

As she entered the room, trying to hold onto her belongings that seemed to be slipping from her hands, my eye was drawn to her worn heels that bore many miles. "She's nervous," I thought to myself as she crossed her legs and began chewing gum in an erratic cadence. After a couple of questions, our interviewee opened one of her torn folders and pulled out her resume. We continued our visit and, just when I thought it couldn't get any worse, she exclaimed she needed a drink and leaned down to the floor to pull out a large cup she had been keeping in her over-sized handbag! Needless to say, she didn't make a good first impression, and she wasn't hired. For the record, I learned that day that you can successfully hide an extra-large Styrofoam cup in a handbag. This is a classic example of losing money because of bad manners.

You are about to enter a room filled with people that you are meeting for the first time, you adjust your jacket, smooth your hair, and secretly tell yourself, "I can do it." That initial entrance can set the tone for how people will be receiving you. Are you wanting to make new friends, win over a potential boss, or gain a client? Choose your strategy and stay on course.

Our world is bringing different personalities, races, and cultures to our neighborhoods and towns. With this ever-pivoting job market and personality tapestry, you need to stand out to form great relationships and compete in business and social situations. People want to be friends with and do business with others they know, trust, and like. Remember, the type of impression you create with new people will help solidify this goal. What are you doing to create a great first impression?

Eye contact is one of the first things you encounter when meeting a new person. Eye contact tells you a lot about a person—are they confident, shy, shifty, or dishonest?

FROZEN IN TIME

There is a saying, "Eyes are the windows to the soul." It means, mostly, people can see through someone else by eye contact in seven seconds. I have a habit that if I meet someone I don't know, I'd like to look at her or his eyes on purpose. When my eyes lay on them, I can immediately see their true color.
- Peng Liyuan

NAVIGATING THE GLACIERS

I once went to an interview with a committee that was being held as an outdoor meeting. Each committee member filed by to introduce themselves, shake hands, and say hello. I was struck by one man who shook my hand and pronounced his name but never took off his sunglasses. My initial impression gave me a funny feeling that he was hiding something or wasn't one hundred percent on board with the meeting. That feeling was affirmed when he later showed his dishonesty and underhandedness in a different setting. Looking back, I realize there was a story to be told with those hiding eyes—he was a shady guy and didn't want his lying eyes to be seen. Don't be guilty of losing money because you tip off a discerning person who knows etiquette and sees you as shady even if you aren't.

<u>**Good Eye Suggestions**</u>

Look someone in the eye. When you are meeting or talking to someone, you want to appear reliable and honest. Hiding your eyes behind designer shades will keep people guessing, and one of the first things you want to do is build trust at the beginning of a new relationship.

Look someone in the eye; we don't trust people who don't show their eyes.

So, you meet someone with a sunspot, zit, or piece of spinach in their teeth! Allow your eyes to see the face as a whole, and try not to let your eyes focus on that lovely facial distraction. After all, you don't want your first encounter to make someone feel self-conscious or uncomfortable.

Facial flaw—look at the face as a whole and turn off condemning eyes.

Ever encountered a person who just stares continually at you, giving you a creepy feeling like they have x-ray vision and are looking into your soul? Unnatural laser-focused eyes don't stir up positive or trusting feelings.

Casually looking at someone with a few blinks and head nods shows you are engaged but not going into a frightening trance.

On one occasion, I was meeting with a woman for a business coffee and noticed she immediately grabbed the seat with her back positioned against the wall. The large public venue was filled with people coming and going in various directions, and I couldn't help but notice her eyes continually followed different individuals as they made their way through the busy common space. Naturally, this type of behavior conveys an attitude that other people and things are more important than the immediate conversation you are engaged in. Needless to say, she did not gain my business or trust.

> *When talking with people in a public or group setting, keep your eyes from following people walking around, noticing others in the room, or simply letting your eyes follow any other moving object in the room. This shows your interest in the person you are speaking with and builds trust.*

We all have encountered that person with sad, puppy dog eyes or angry eyes that can immediately turn a conversation or first impression into a negative spiral. Try smiling with your eyes.

> *Slightly raising your eyebrows, thinking of something good, and relaxing your face and jaw can convey smiling eyes. Smile with your eyes.*

Have you ever experienced a sarcastic teenager or aggressive business tyrant who rolled their eyes when hearing information they didn't like? (Side note: you probably aren't going to get skinny practicing your eye roll muscles; be more productive and work on abs or legs!) This type of behavior can give the impression that the person talking is giving ridiculous information, creating a negative conversation.

> *Drum roll please (actually, eye roll)! Practice a calm facial expression with soothing eyes, eyebrows relaxed, and eyeballs steady, not rolling your eyes out of frustration and revealing your disapproval of this new information.*

Don't you just love it when someone looks you up and down with approval like you are wearing a great outfit? What about that up and down look conveys they are thinking, "I can't believe you wore that?"

> *When approaching someone, keep eye contact with the person you are meeting, and don't become an instant fashion critic with the up and down eye movement or a look of condemnation.*

Try to establish a confident impression using your eye. We've all seen the chastised child or self-conscious adult who looks down due to low self-esteem or self-confidence. This speaks of feeling insecure, and who wants to hire an insecure, unsuccessful person?

> *Even if you aren't feeling super confident in a conversation, maintain eye contact and occasionally look away to the side, not down. A continual downward eye glance could indicate your lack of confidence.*

Eye contact is viewed differently in different countries. Male-to-female eye contact in certain countries isn't the norm, so knowing your location can be extremely beneficial in business or relational settings. I once visited a country where the female was expected to not look a man in the eyes, which I respected due to their customs. But in the United States, there is a different norm. If you are a female, feel confident when looking a man in the eye; it builds respect. Discernment and knowledge are of importance on this subject.

> *When visiting a different country, learn about their social norms and respect them. In the United States, look everyone in the eye confidently and engage in a great conversation. If you have recently moved from a different country, learn about US social norms so you can create a positive impression and engage in business.*

Ever been in a conversation where the person speaking only engaged in eye contact with one person in the group? Or have you listened to a speaker who seemed to look past his audience so as not to make eye contact? Several people come to mind when I think of this. This might indicate the person feels insecure or uncomfortable speaking with certain genders or cultures. This can easily make the person listening spiral into other questions, distracting from the topic at hand.

> *Pleasantly engaging in eye contact with everyone in the conversation shows involvement and possibly confidence.*

<u>Body Language</u>

Nonverbal behavior is the most crucial element of communication. Studies by Dr. Albert Mehrabian indicate that 55% of communication is conveyed through facial expressions, gestures, and posture;

38% is conveyed through tone; and only 7% comes through words.
2

FROZEN IN TIME

I would also say that nonverbal skills are even more important now than they were before this global pandemic. It's my belief that anyone who develops strong nonverbal communication skills in today's "new normal" world is going to reap significant rewards in both the short-term and long-term future.
- Jon Michail

NAVIGATING THE GLACIERS

Years ago, my husband and I traveled to Brazil with a group of people and quickly learned about Brazilian customs, greetings, etc. One of our traveling companions missed one of the key meetings and wasn't clued in on some of the differences in body language in the US versus Brazil. Missing this one session proved to be quite humorous for us but insulting to our Brazilian hosts. Body language can tell you a lot about a person and their self-confidence, habits, likes, dislikes, and overall knowledge on different subjects. Even though we had translators, the language created a slight barrier at times. At a dinner hosted by our Brazilian friends, our American teammate wanted to indicate the meal was good by flashing the Brazilians an okay symbol, which is generally accepted as a good sign in the US. While getting shocked looks from our Brazilian friends, our team had to quickly let him know that he had just insulted our hosts with body language that was the same as giving the finger in the United States. There wasn't any laughing at the moment, but to this day, we laugh about it and remind him of the proper way to communicate through body language without insulting anyone! Remember your rules of etiquette and body language before encountering others so you don't lose an initial interview, resulting in a loss of money.

Since the first seven seconds of a first impression are important and fifty-five percent of your communication is made through body language, thinking through your entrance into a room might be important. Like making a grand entrance onto a stage (think rock star or supermodel), take the time to adjust your clothing, make sure zippers are zipped, hair is in place, and all excess lunch is removed from your face. Are you trying to appear confident or weak and unsure?

As in the military or a marching band, the command, "Attention!" snaps members into an upright position with shoulders back and chin up. This stance usually indicates the person is in position, confident, and ready to go. As a former drum major, I would utilize this command to get everyone's attention with eyes focused on the front and bodies positioned correctly for an entrance. This might be a great idea to remember before making your grand entrance. Walking in with your shoulders back, head up, and eyes forward shows you are confidently marching in for success with your potential new client, friend, relative, or audience. Chances are great that your potential clients want to work with a confident person, leaving more money in your pocket.

<u>**Are You Giving the Cold Shoulder?**</u>

We've probably all encountered the timid person who tries to slip quietly into a room half crouching, with shoulders down, and walking quietly. This person doesn't want any attention and could come across as meek, versus the boisterous person who bounds through the door with broad shoulders and a booming voice drawing everyone's attention.

Try entering a room with shoulders back and head up with an air of confidence—not arrogant or obnoxious—but to create a great first impression, ready to win new clients and friends.

While conversing with someone, take note of shoulder height—shrugging can indicate a lack of knowledge or understanding.

To give the impression of understanding or comprehension, practice keeping your shrugs to a minimum.

Your mother probably taught you to keep your shoulders up, or perhaps a physical therapist urged you to remember to sit up straight. These are great reminders especially if you aren't overly confident and find yourself with slouched shoulders. Remember, gaining trust is key and body language is an important part of that.

Even if you aren't a confident person, practice keeping your shoulders rolled back so you appear confident and engaged.

<u>**Need a Hand Out or a Leg Up?**</u>

Unsure of what to do with your hands when approaching a person or entering a room? Try keeping your hands out of your pockets so you don't look insecure and keep your palms up in a comfortable, relaxed position.

Keeping your palms up indicates trustworthiness, honesty, and your willingness to connect.

After you've made your entrance and engaged in conversation, how are you maintaining that positive impression? Beautiful hair is great but can become a distraction and give off a flirty or distracting vibe if twirling becomes your obsession during a conversation.

Try to remain focused on your subject matter and keep your hands out of your lovely locks of hair.

What's your stance saying about you? If you stand slouched over, your shoulders rolled forward, and your head glancing downward, you appear insecure.

While engaging in a new conversation, stand with feet apart, shoulders back, and head erect to indicate confidence.

Are you cold or just angry? Oftentimes we see people with their arms crossed to keep warm, or maybe there is something that ticked them off. What are you saying with your arms?

Uncross and be less cross. Conversing with people with arms down or not crossed makes you appear open to them and perpetuates positive reception.

Everyone wants to be hip (at least in the 60s), but it comes with a price. Standing with your hands on your hips can appear too aggressive.

Try standing with your hands by your side instead of striking a Superman pose with your hands on your hips.

Still don't know what to do with your hands while standing and talking or waiting on stage for an award? The fig leaf position (which subconsciously hides private parts) tends to be a default position for most people just a little anxious or unsure, which can give off the wrong impression.

Once again, appear confident and open with hands to the side or hands clasped casually behind your back with your head up. And act confident even if you don't feel it.

Have you ever been asked for directions? Avoid giving the finger—the pointer finger that is. An aggressive one-finger point with intentional positioning can come across as too aggressive or uncaring.

If you are pointing out something to someone or giving directions, point with the entire hand and not just the pointer finger. Better yet, if you are close to what the person is looking for, don't just point it out: walk them over to it.

Personal Space

Personal space is the distance between two people when talking and is different in many cultures.

FROZEN IN TIME

In the Middle East, social distance is closer than it is in the United States, so as you back up, your conversational partner may attempt to close the gap once again.
~ Roger Kreuz and Richard Roberts [3]

NAVIGATING THE GLACIERS

Years ago, my husband and I were on vacation and decided to visit a famous chocolate factory. While touring the factory, we were suddenly invaded by a tour bus full of foreign visitors who practice different rules regarding personal space. We immediately found ourselves standing elbow to elbow, having our personal space invaded. I'll never forget the uncomfortable feeling of having a stranger within a couple of inches, if not touching, at times. My husband who is 6'5" also became uncomfortable and jokingly said he was tempted to bend down and scare all of them. Needless to say, we left the business and didn't make any purchases but regained our personal space. Are you aware of your personal space within other cultures?

Knowing what your present culture dictates as the norm is key: you can easily be misunderstood with improper personal space. We probably all know that close talker who makes us unconsciously begin to back up. No one likes to have their personal space invaded.

Be respectful of personal space and become familiar with the cultural norms where you are. The important thing to remember is to make the other person feel comfortable, so you might need to adjust to accommodate them. There are some countries where people do not have a lot of personal space at all. For example, people who live in Bulgaria, Peru, and Argentina are known to stand very close to strangers. When people walk down the street in these countries, it is not unusual for people to stand right next to strangers as they walk. There are even some situations where they may bump into one another. When standing in line, people who live in these countries also do not give a lot of space between them and the person in front of them. There is not a lot of personal space available when people go to visit these countries. [4]

And there are a few countries where people stand far apart from one another.

For example, people who live in Romania, Hungary, and Saudi Arabia are known to stand relatively far apart from the people around them. They like to give people more space to operate. Regarding the United States, Americans are somewhere in the middle. There are some locations where people in the US tend to give a lot of space to strangers walking down the street, but there are other situations where Americans might feel more like sardines. [5]

<u>**Sounds & Suggestions**</u>

People with misophonia, the condition of being easily annoyed with everyday sounds, can quickly divert attention away from the conversation or business deal.

Try not to tap fingernails, juggle keys, click a pen, or make other small irritating noises when conversing. After all, you are trying to build positive rapport.

<u>**Shaking Hands**</u>

In a post-pandemic world, this one gesture has caused much conversation. The idea to remember is that you are trying to greet people and instill trust and confidence so you can create a positive client, personal, or business relationship. As I mentioned in the first part of this book, discernment is key. You may need to practice the skill of discernment before moving forward. During the height of the pandemic, people were scared to sneeze in public much less shake hands. Now that the pandemic has been officially deemed over, this action may still win over a client or friend, or it could have the opposite; proceed cautiously and thoughtfully.

The handshake is a normal greeting in the US and is exchanged with both men and women. Years ago, it was considered rude for a man to extend his hand to a woman, but these days it is proper, acceptable, and expected for both men and women to initiate a handshake. Make sure to offer your hand of greeting to everyone you are meeting; you never know who the decision maker is in the group, and you don't want to start a meeting offending someone.

Shaking hands is common sense—everyone knows how

to do this. Or do they? I've heard this comment many times, so a few years ago before presenting this topic at a conference, I stood at the back of the room and had thirty highly-educated businessmen and women with degrees slowly file into the conference room. I decided to see how many people knew how to shake hands properly. Amazingly, only one out of thirty knew how to properly shake hands. (Coincidentally, they were all attending the class because their businesses were suffering, but they didn't know why their initial impressions of people were failing.)

What Makes a Good Handshake?

When shaking hands, grab hands at the joint, keep arms parallel to the floor, and firmly (not limp but not too firm) pump twice, release, and step back out of their personal space. Don't turn your hand over so your hand is on top and parallel to the floor.

This shows dominance and aggression, a trait you probably don't want to convey at an initial meeting. If someone does this to you, watch out! You may be dealing with a pushy person.

Conversely, what does it mean when you shake hands with someone and they immediately turn their hand palm up and parallel to the floor?

This might be a less confident, non-aggressive client who allows others to push them around. Make them feel warm and accepted by turning your hand so that both are perpendicular to the floor, creating an equal environment.

If you are meeting for the first time, your goal is to have a positive greeting but not too invasive.

Shake hands normally as mentioned above and avoid the two-handed shake, meaning one hand pumping and the other grabbing the person's arm at the same time. This first-time handshake is deemed too personal; a two-handed shake on the next visit might be more appropriate.

Who goes first?

Typically, the higher-ranking individual offers a handshake first, but if they don't, remember the old song, "Shake a Hand, Shake a Hand" by Dean Martin and Jerry Lewis. It's a business greeting, and it should be initiated by someone. Take charge and get it done!

I'm at a party; what about my drink?

Try to be proactive and keep your drink, food, or keys in your left hand with your right hand ready to meet and greet. The last-minute shuffling of things from your right to left hand can come across as awkward, and you never know who your next client might be.

What if someone high-fives me?

If they initiated it, go ahead and follow through—after all, you are welcoming and trying to create a positive vibe. If you are the first to greet someone, go old school and extend a hand. You may be subconsciously telling someone they are germy and dirty if you initiate a high-five.

What if you are a man extending your hand to an older lady, and she doesn't reciprocate?

This may be an older person who is unaware of updated etiquette rules. Brush it off and proceed. Create a welcoming introduction and remind yourself that you still have the job of creating a positive first impression.

You initiate a handshake with someone and suddenly you realize they have a hand deformity.

Keep eye contact and follow through with an in-motion handshake as normal so as not to embarrass or slight the new friend.

You are out and about town, and you meet someone who extends their left hand to you instead of their right.

Make them feel at ease with you. You aren't their mother there to correct them. Shake with your left hand—they may have a hand injury and are playing it safe.

You are having a wonderful meal at a restaurant, and someone approaches your table to say hello and extends their hand as a warm gesture.

Always stand to greet and shake hands. If you are trapped in a booth and find it difficult to stand, make the effort of half-standing, showing your respect to the greeter.

Have you ever initiated a handshake and missed hands or grabbed only a portion of the other person's hand?

Remember, you are trying to create a warm first impression, so if this happens, play it off, laugh at yourself, make a joke, and keep going. You may accidentally make an instant new friend, and they will know you have a sense of humor and can creatively manage life.

If you are traveling to another country, get ahead of the curve and learn the culture's greeting norms.

A handshake or greeting is performed differently in different countries. What works in one country may be an insult in another. For example, in Russia people greet and shake hands but not over a threshold, which could be considered bad luck. In Italy, shake hands with everyone in the room and allow the women to offer their hands first.

Want to shake hands and come across as up-front and honest?

Shake hands with people while keeping your other hand out of your pocket. A hidden hand could appear sneaky or suspicious like you are recording or getting ready to pull a weapon.

You want to give positive information to a client?

Rubbing your palms together can give the expectation that you are about to give exciting news. This might be a positive setup for salespeople setting up a great purchase scenario.

<u>**What's That Smell?**</u>

FROZEN IN TIME

Smelling good is like having a personal fan club—people just can't help but be drawn to you.
~ Gabriel Cruz[6]

Smells go a long way toward making a good first impression or keeping a positive one. Smells tell a lot about a person or organization. Does your company use a cheap cleaner? (I won't mention names here, but you know who you are.) Smells can also be a trigger for people's childhood memories (good and bad), the remembrances of your high school locker room, fresh spring flowers, or a gentle breeze wafting through your house with the windows open in good weather. What smelly impressions are you giving off?

Nothing is more memorable than a smell. One scent can be unexpected, momentary and fleeting, yet conjure up a childhood summer beside a lake in the mountains.
~ Diane Ackerman

"Scents can influence people's emotions, so they have the potential to affect consumer behavior," says Melissa Sanfilippo, contributing writer at Business News Daily.[7]

Moreover, smell is the most powerful and emotional of all the senses. By using scent, brands can connect with consumers on a deeper emotional level, resulting in a more memorable experience. Scent can attract new customers,

increase sales, heighten value perception, and expand
brand recognition and customer satisfaction. A scent can
influence behavior and trigger memories almost instanta-
neously. When smell is combined with other marketing
cues, it can amplify a brand experience and establish a
long-lasting connection with consumers.[8]

NAVIGATING THE GLACIERS

Years ago, I had an experience with a lady who was in a
musical group that I was associated with. She was extremely
sensitive to certain perfumes and was quick to let everyone
around her know. Her demeanor was arrogant and entitled
when she demanded everyone in the group not use any
scented products when she was present. Naturally, her
demanding personality turned a lot of people off and irritated those who wore pleasant scents. This lady eventually
alienated most people around her because of her demeanor,
and she ended up leaving the musical organization.

If you are trying to build trust and confidence, the way
you approach people is vital in getting your message across.
This lady could have politely let the director or those
around her know about her condition, coming across in a
polite tone and hopefully encouraging those around her to
tone down the perfumes. But her barking attitude did just
the opposite.

On the flip side, I knew an administrative assistant years
ago who had severe allergies to scents, and her entire
approach was different. She politely let everyone know
about her situation, and when she lost her voice and became
severely congested on a few occasions, people immediately
wanted to help her and were considerate in their fragrance
selections. She naturally created a positive spirit regarding

this subject and was a friend to many versus the lady in the choir who demanded she get her way. If you are trying to win people over, think about your approach and what etiquette suggests for creating positive connections.

There is a condition known as hyperosmia, which is a hypersensitivity to smells and can be triggered or heightened by pregnancy, allergies, Lyme disease, genetics, and autoimmune disease. Your job isn't to cater to everyone with sensitivities, but making yourself aware of such things might help make a great first impression, understanding your friends and colleagues, and setting yourself up for success with as many people as possible. You would hate to lose money because of your demeanor when dealing with others and your sense of smell.

Wanting to create a great first impression with possible new clients entering your office or house?

Think about and do your research to find pleasant smells that will evoke a pleasant memory so that they will think of your brand when they encounter the pleasant smell again. According to The Healthy, *a* Readers Digest *brand newsletter, these eight scents can make you happier and may be helpful to remember when implementing scents into your office or workplace to create happy vibes: pine, citrus, sunscreen, fresh cut grass, flowers, rosemary, peppermint, and baby powder.[9] Be sure to utilize whatever scent you choose in moderation. The use of plants, natural cleaning products, and proper ventilation can also help.*

Are you entertaining potential clients by hosting a dinner and want to win them over?

As we all know, that initial meeting is key, and scents play an important role. As with anything in etiquette, play it conservatively by cooking food that doesn't give off a possible offensive odor. Broccoli, cauliflower, and roasted Brussels sprouts are great for a healthy diet and taste wonderful, but they may turn off your first-time guests with their strong aroma.

You are on a plane or in a small cubicle and have a craving for and happen to have a container of oily tuna fish. Seems perfectly innocent right?

Be cognizant and courteous with those around you in tight spots so your innocent food preference isn't turning others off, raising eyebrows, or making them sick. Let's face it, you probably won't be gaining many friends with a strong food odor; save these delicious morsels for open-air areas or larger venues.

Lying through your teeth does not count as flossing.
- Anonymous

Dental health isn't a laughing matter (no, my dentist isn't paying me to talk dental), and those around you thank you for flossing and brushing often.

There's nothing worse than talking with someone with bad breath; so brush, floss, and keep mints handy if necessary.

Teenage boys after football practice, a high school gym, you after a hot summer day, some things go without saying...

Always be generous with your time, your affection, and your deodorant.

Mother's Sunday pot roast, movie popcorn, and fine leather—all these things may evoke positive feelings. If so, remember to utilize the sense of smell properly in your business and social settings to benefit you and create a positive memory with future clients, friends, and colleagues.

May I Introduce...

Introductions to new people are important when beginning a conversation. After you've entered a room using appropriate eye contact and body language, a proper introduction will be vital in forming a positive first impression for a new client, friend, or colleague. If you have dressed the part, walked the walk, and given off a confident vibe, it's time to open up and talk.

FROZEN IN TIME

Your tone of voice encompasses your words. It's how you speak and the lasting impression words make on everyone around you. Think of your tone of voice like a personalized vocal "fingerprint" that distinguishes who you are and can tell others so much about you.

NAVIGATING THE GLACIERS

We have a term in our house we like to use—bubble talk—when we get ready to talk but forget to clear our throat first. Without doing so, our voices can sound raspy and unclear.

I was in a coffee shop recently and saw a well-dressed businessman ready to order. What caught my attention was his tone of voice when he placed his order. Instead of sounding confident with his selection, the man had begun talking without clearing his throat so it came across as a meager request—bubble talk. It almost made me laugh out loud—a professional-looking, confident man dressed to the nines blew his first impression because he hadn't cleared his throat before speaking. He sounded like Woody Woodpecker when he started talking. If that had been a business deal, it may have made the client question who he was doing business with—a known cartoon character?

You are ready to talk; what's next?

Before speaking, analyze the situation you are in, clear your voice if needed, and begin speaking. Do you need a formal, informal, serious, confident, or respectful tone? When meeting a potential client, you will need a confident yet respectful tone. By the way, no bubble talk here!

Are you a quiet talker?

Make sure to speak clearly when introducing yourself; you want people to know your name and not guess if you are Ronny or Randy.

Back before cell phones and caller ID, there were times I would answer the phone, and the caller would start talking without identifying themselves. Not wanting to sound cold, I would engage in the conversation while trying to figure out who I was talking to. This has probably happened to you, too.

Because of social media, people might start talking to you because they have seen you on their devices and assume a comfort level even when you have no clue who they are. Here are a few ways to handle that situation.

You are meeting someone for the first time; what should you do?

Look the new person in the eye, extend your hand, smile, get your proper tone ready, and say, "I don't believe we've met; my name is..."

Someone approaches you in a restaurant; what is the norm?

Always stand to show courtesy when greeting someone. There may be times when you are caught in a booth or behind a counter, but you can show politeness by making a half-stand to greet the person.

Someone approaches you while you are in a group.

After the person has greeted you, it is polite for you to introduce your friends if the person initiating the conversation hasn't already done so.

Who do you introduce first—your boss or your client?

Since you are creating a positive environment, always introduce the most important person first. In this scenario, the client is the most important. "I would like to introduce you to my boss…"

Want to introduce your boss to a colleague?

The same rule applies here: the most important person is introduced first. For example, "Mr. Boss, meet Mrs. Jones. She works in another area of our company."

What about titles when introducing someone?

In a formal setting, always introduce someone by their title. It's best to err on the conservative side if you are unsure. For example, "Dr. Jones, I'd like to introduce you to Mr. Smith."

Introducing a child to an adult?
Reinforce respect with the child and positive feelings with the adult. For example, "Mrs. Anthony, meet my son Billy."

Introducing an adult to a friend?

Always introduce the older to the younger. For example, "Grandfather, meet Julie my friend from school."

Help, I can't remember her name!

It happens to everyone; you have forgotten your neighbor's name and you are about to introduce them to your friend who has dropped in. Be honest and simply say something like, "Oh my, I've gone blank, remind me of your name." Play it off, make a joke, and move on. It's a normal thing that happens to everyone. The important thing is that you are introducing everyone.

Your Clothes Make an Impression, Too

You've got seconds to make that great first impression, and of course, your clothing and accessories can make or break you. You don't have to be a designer, supermodel, or even wear the most expensive clothes; knowing how to dress appropriately is the key. You probably wouldn't wear a swimsuit to a wedding or a bridal gown to the beach, and the same thing applies to business meetings versus a casual lunch—know what is appropriate. The key thing to remember is that it is better to be the best dressed in the room (within reason) if you are wondering what to wear. It has been said that you should dress for the job you want and not the job you have. This is a key element when dressing for any occasion. If you walk into a meeting wearing sneakers and jeans while everyone else is wearing suits and heels, you probably aren't going to make a great first impression. And chances are, you will feel self-conscious, which will be seen in your posture as you carry yourself throughout the day.

FROZEN IN TIME

It is important to choose our dress style carefully because people will make all sorts of assumptions and decisions about us without proper evidence.
~ Ben Fletcher[11]

Dressing well is a form of good manners.
~ Tom Ford

NAVIGATING THE GLACIERS

Years ago, I had a friend whose husband was a CEO. She was attending a dinner with her husband's clients. She assumed it was a casual event, so she wore her best denim dress and casual shoes. Much to her horror, everyone was wearing business and cocktail attire—some women even wore mink stoles and glittery diamond jewelry. She immediately felt out of place, and her body language showed it. She learned a hard lesson that day: do a little investigation ahead of time to find out the dress code. As the CEO's wife, she needed to be one of the best dressed in the room to make a good impression. That power couple didn't take their leadership roles seriously and neither did their clients and staff. This was just one of the many things that led to their demise, and they were asked to leave the job after a couple of years.

How you dress is just one element of the impression you are giving. Go the extra mile and find out the attire before an event so you aren't losing money because of a careless wardrobe error.

Have you looked at your shoes and heels recently?

Believe it or not, you will be judged by your shoes. Make sure you don't have scraped heels or dusty loafers. Invest in nice shoes and/or find a good shoe repair person.

To reveal or not reveal

Doing a little homework on attire is never a bad idea. Know your audience. If you are walking into a conservative bank meeting or interview, dress accordingly with nothing revealing or distracting. This probably won't be the atmosphere to wear that mini skirt or new blouse with a plunging neckline.

Sporty versus business

Skip the athletic shorts and wear slacks if you are meeting the bank president for an interview. Sounds like common sense, but common sense doesn't seem to be common sometimes.

Trying a new restaurant, attending the theater or visiting a club?

Call ahead (or look at the website) and ask about collared shirts and jackets; otherwise, you might end up wearing a non-matching, musty, courtesy jacket. Or you could be refused entry for not having the proper attire.

Meeting scheduled but you stop to eat first

If you are a sloppy eater or just want to play it safe, avoid spaghetti, coffee, and other messy foods. A stained blouse or slacks will set you apart but not in a good way.

What are your wrinkles saying?

Unless you are discussing age or materials designed with certain textures, press on, my friend and take out the wrinkles to make a great first impression. This shows you take time for details, look sharp, and are ready to go.

Ripped, torn, and frayed edges—what's the best option?

Ripped jeans with frayed edges are all the rage in certain areas and can be seen as quite stylish, but in a business-to-formal atmosphere, they can become a distraction. When meeting a new possible client, know your audience ahead of time and dress appropriately. You don't want to give the impression you are a slob or don't pay attention to detail.

Does the color of my clothes matter?

If you want to dress for business, wear black, blue, brown, or grey. Black is seen as the color of sophistication, mystery, power, and control, whereas "yellow is seen as the least attractive color on both men and women." [12] *Choose your colors appropriately.*

Hair today and gone tomorrow.

When you are meeting someone for the first time, your hair makes a statement for you; you wouldn't want to scare off a new friend or client because you didn't pay attention to your locks of love. There are many styles, colors, and shapes that are appropriate for different settings, but one thing to keep in mind is to make sure your hair is clean, neat, and not distracting. If you are going for the sexy, wind-blown, or grunge look, save it for the appropriate time, which isn't the office or traditional networking meetings. And remember to check your hair in a mirror before going into a meeting.

Nailed it...or maybe not.

Take time to clean, file, and maintain your nails. Since a first impression is made in seconds, people will notice little things like dirty, jagged, discolored, half-painted nails, which could give off a negative vibe before you even open your mouth to speak. Don't forget your toenails in the summertime when you are sporting open-toed shoes!

APPLY ICE

One time I was asked to speak to a group of professionals about first impressions, and as I was walking into the building, one of my heel protectors popped off, leaving me with one shoe taller than the other. I learned then to create an emergency impressions kit and keep it handy. Thankfully, I was able to fix my shoe and walk into the conference with confidence. But to this day, I keep a spare set of shoes in my car and an emergency kit for such situations.

<u>Sample Emergency Kit</u>

- **Deodorant**: If you live in an area that experiences extreme heat, we all ask that you carry deodorant.
- **Breath mints**: Go ahead and enjoy your garlic toast at lunch, but if you want to win over a new client, you might think about freshening up your breath. According to Listerine, the top five foods that cause bad breath are garlic, onions, dairy, canned tuna, and horseradish.
- **Fingernail file**: You might think of the most obvious use for this, but it can also double as a scraper for the bottom of your shoes if they are new and slippery. After all, you don't want to go sliding into your meeting.
- **Needle/thread**: Gained a little weight and your clothes are stretching at the seams or a button decides to take a hike? Be prepared so you aren't embarrassed.
- **Lint brush:** Black slacks and your waiter at lunch gave you a white cloth napkin? Enough said.
- **Hairbrush:** Unless you are still living in the 60s with hair-sprayed, back-combed hair, always be prepared with a brush.
- **Dry shampoo:** A little spritz of this will refresh your day-two hair and give volume at the same time.

- **Hand mirror**: Even your best friend might have
  a hard time telling you that you've got pepper in
  your teeth, or, worse, something sticking out of
  your nose.
- **Stain stick**: Spaghetti got away from you? If you
  don't have a backup shirt, make like a magician
  and make the stain disappear.
- **Super glue:** You never know when your heel
  might break.
- **Extra pair of shoes:** I wear "parking lot shoes"
  from the car into a meeting or work. An extra
  pair of shoes can help avoid a crisis.
- **Disinfecting wipes**: Post-pandemic, no need to
  explain this one.
- **Paper towels:** If you haven't stashed every
  drive-through napkin in your car by now, keep a
  few handy.
- **Dryer sheets:** Sweaty shoes, static cling, or
  removing deodorant stains are just a few uses for
  this emergency tool.
- **Natural ways to eliminate odors:** Baking
  soda, coffee grounds, vinegar, and tea bags are all-
  natural products that can be left out to eliminate
  odors in tight spaces. Washing all clothes in the
  suitcase after a trip, worn or not worn, also helps
  freshen things up.

Chapter Three

COMMUNICATION

TURN MANNERS INTO MONEY WITHOUT FREEZING UP

FROZEN IN TIME

A good bedside manner is far more effective at reducing the risk of medical malpractice litigation than common practices of ordering excessive tests and procedures, sometimes called "defensive medicine," The New York Times *reported. The patients seeing doctors who faced the most malpractice lawsuits—not only the ones who actually filed those suits—felt that these doctors ignored them, rushed them or failed to explain things adequately. Frequently sued doctors are the subject of twice as many complaints as doctors without such a troubled history. Most often, complaints referenced the doctor's poor communication.*
- Richard P. Console, Jr.[1]

Communication is vital in every industry, so turn your manners into money with different forms of communication.

NAVIGATING THE GLACIERS

One time I made arrangements with a friend to meet for lunch at a local chain restaurant. I arranged my day around the location of this favorite restaurant and arrived early to get us a table. After waiting some time, I began to get a little concerned when my friend Susan didn't arrive. I had other appointments that day, and my time was limited, so I gave her a call. Much to my chagrin, Susan was waiting at a table at the restaurant we had decided upon, but at a different location. We had failed to communicate properly about one very important detail.

Communication comes in many forms, especially in our post-pandemic world where so much is online, but one thing is certain: to gain more clients, make more friends, and create pleasant comradery in the office, it is important that communication exists and is performed effectively. Communication exists in every aspect of life. From the early days of stone and chisel to Zoom, texting, and Face-time, it is important to understand and participate in proper communication to succeed in everyday life.

After making a good first impression, shaking hands, and making introductions, it is now time to engage in good communication and conversation. Making natural, appropriate conversation is an art and can be the difference between gaining a new client and losing out. You may have the best product or service in the world, but don't lose money because you simply don't know how to communicate effectively.

Let's Talk

FROZEN IN TIME

A single conversation across a table with a wise man is better than ten years mere study of books.
~ Henry Wadsworth Longfellow

NAVIGATING THE GLACIERS

Years ago, we had a house in a large circular subdivision with many neighbors of different ages, occupations, and ethnicities. We had two white rockers on the front porch, which we used frequently when visiting with neighbors or just relaxing. That front porch became the conversation starter with so many people on different occasions. Being able to relate to, converse, and form relationships with people of different ages—from teens to senior adults—is so important. Little did I know that the variety of those conversations would lead to lifelong friends, great neighbors, and even clients. We all got to know each other, told our stories, and, over time, valued our trusted relationships.

Unless you live under a rock in a desolate area, chances are you will need to know how to converse with different people in different settings. Perfecting your conversation skills can make you stand out positively in business, social settings, or everyday life. There is an art to knowing how to navigate conversations effectively with senior adults, teenagers, peers, long talkers, narcissists, negative people, etc. You can be an extrovert or introvert and still know how to engage in general conversations effectively to gain more clients and friends, or ease office tensions.

How do you engage in general conversation?

When striking up a conversation with someone for the first time, take time to listen to the individual, and pick up on clues as to common hobbies, foods, vocations, etc., so you can carry on the dialogue. Develop the habit of noticing non-controversial bill-boards, news stories, or sports teams, and read new books so you can discuss positive current events and subjects, kicking off a great dialogue. If you find out the person you are talking with has grandkids, talk about grandkids. The key is to listen and casually notice common points of interest so you can connect. Stay away from controversial subjects like religion and politics. You are trying to earn trust, so avoid controversial topics so you don't sabo-tage future communication.

Need to get out of a conversation?

We have all been trapped in a conversation where we need to make a quick exit for various reasons but don't want to offend the other person. Wait for a break in the conversation and politely thank the person for their time and make a wrap-up comment such as, "It has been good visiting with you; thank you for your time."

Are you with a long-winded talker?

Some will use 2,000 words to explain a 200-word story, and this can be frustrating when you have a busy schedule or get over-whelmed with so many extra words. Gently redirect the conversa-tion to the subject at hand and say something like, "Let me make sure I understand what you said." If the person responds with a yes or no answer, make your break politely. If they continue to talk, use your body language by slowly gathering your things and standing up or slowly moving toward the door while wrapping up. Make sure to end the conversation with a polite "thank you" or "see you later" before making your exit.

Are you a Tammy or Tommy Top It?

Have you ever told a story about a great trip or recent award only to have someone jump in with a story about their recent award or trip, directing the conversation toward themselves and leaving you out of the conversation or downplaying your experience? There will always be the Tammy or Tommy Top It who loves to talk about themselves. Make sure you listen to other people's stories and don't bring up your own experiences unless asked to do so. If you experience this scenario with an interrupter, listen politely then circle back and finish your story. Wise, well-trained people in the room will recognize and take note of your polished communication skills.

What's the rule about interrupting?

If you are trying to gain clients, maintain good conversation, or make a great first impression, limit interruptions. Interrupting someone during a conversation can give the impression that you are bossy, uncaring, or not well-versed in manners when conversing with people. It may also appear inpatient, lacking polish or education. It may be hard to do, but listen to the complete conversation then give your response when appropriate.

What about the person who keeps interrupting you in conversation?

You may be polished and aware of the rule of interrupting, but when encountering someone who keeps interrupting, keeping your demeanor is key. If someone keeps interrupting you, complete your sentence in a normal tone with a nice countenance. It is important to not elevate your voice, which is easy to do if you are trying to talk over someone. The best way to avoid a conversation becoming heated is to listen when they are speaking and reply in a calm voice, even if they begin to talk loudly over you.

Communicating with confidence

If you are asked a question in a social or professional setting, speak with confidence (only if you know the answer) and state the facts. For example, "The vote is in, and you are now the new president of the club," or "The cause of your computer failure is due to your hard drive." In both cases, you have stated verified information. Avoid looking weak by using the phrase, "I think."

Hello, Sweetie Pie...

We've all encountered that teenager behind the counter who addresses someone as "Honey" or the local waitress who refers to everyone as "Sweetie." Terms of endearment like sweetie, honey, baby, etc., are also known as hypocorisms. *The use of these terms can be interpreted as condescending. Avoid using them and possibly offending your future clients, friends, relatives, and others. Call them by name and reinforce your positive reception of them.*

You've forgotten someone's name.

Chances are great that everyone has been in a position where they forgot someone's name. What do you do? Be honest and upfront and say something like, "I've gone blank; remind me of your name please."

You want to be able to remember someone's name

There are different methods you can use to remember someone's name. Remembering people's names can help you gain a new client, retain a friend, or make someone feel known. Try repeating the other person's name several times in conversation. Keep a list of names in your phone after attending a party, or associate their name with something easy to remember. For example, a friend of mine has the last name Cook, and he happens to be a chef. Pretty easy to remember that one.

Mingling in a crowd, party, reception, or networking event

The important thing to remember when conversing at a social event is to make a lasting positive impression. This may involve briefly speaking to different people in the room, not dominating any one person, choosing non-controversial subject matter, and keeping your conversations to a minimum to be sensitive to others in the room.

Are you a detail talker?

Going into details about your trip, describing every road you took, or every meal you ate will probably cause you to lose your audience in seconds. Remember to limit details to the important information to keep your conversation informative. Don't give your audience the chance to daydream or slip away.

Too personal?

Remember, your audience may not have a strong stomach or a bold sense of adventure. In other words, keep your recent surgery details and horror stories to a minimum. Some people may be turned off by your recent bowel surgery or colonoscopy preparation.

Getting out of a conversation when it's not the right time to talk

When you engage someone in conversation and realize they have something heavy going on, by all means, pivot and excuse yourself so you can talk another time. You won't win friends and new clients by talking about your new award while the person you are talking to has just experienced a death or job loss. Make a polite comment like, "Let's talk another time," or "I realize this isn't a good time; let's catch up later."

<u>Disagree With Grace</u>

FROZEN IN TIME
He who cannot put his thoughts on ice should not enter into the heat of dispute.
- Friedrich Nietzsche

NAVIGATING THE GLACIERS

I recently attended a large business meeting, which allowed for discussion about a controversial subject that was to be voted on after people were allowed to express their points of view. The people voting in favor of the subject matter spoke with a pleasant tone of voice, calm body language, and a smile on their faces. The opposite was true when the opposing side was allowed to speak. There was an angry tone of voice, tense body language, and angry eyes. Those who agreed with the speaker cheered, but they booed and hissed when the other side spoke. It was obvious the stress level in the room increased greatly when the heated speaker continued and encouraged negative behavior. Much anger and high blood pressure could have been avoided if strategies had been used to avoid a mob scene and negative impressions. I still remember seeing several individuals acting inappropriately, and I determined I would never do business with them due to their lack of self-control and nasty behavior. Think about the impression you are giving to bystanders when you disagree in a childlike manner. You may be losing trust and money without even knowing it.

Ready to disagree?

Whether in a small or large group, the idea is the same: disagree with confidence but without inciting people. Keep your voice strong and steady, keep to a slower pace, avoid a high pitch, keep something in your hand if you're prone to swinging your arms wildly, smile periodically, keep your points on track, avoid absolutes like always and never, and encourage positive behavior with your support group. Remind others to avoid booing and hissing and model a positive mindset.

Possible silence

Social Media

FROZEN IN TIME

"Build it, and they will come" only works in the movies. Social Media is a "build it, nurture it, engage them, and they may come and stay."
- Seth Godin [2]

Social media, like Facebook, X, Instagram, Pinterest, and LinkedIn, have transformed business and personal communication. It's not uncommon to attend a convention or event and run into someone you haven't spoken with in years, but they congratulate you on your most recent accomplishment or ask about your family vacation due to information they saw on social media. Having all types of information for the public to see is sometimes startling when you speak with that long-lost friend to only find out that they have been watching you closely throughout the years. Social media can be a great tool if used properly but can damage your reputation if not paid attention to.

NAVIGATING THE GLACIERS

Social media can have a positive or negative impact, depending on how you use it. Knowing, thinking through, and implementing basic courtesies on social media is a must. One time I was presenting on a relatively high platform with audience members below. During my presentation, one of the members of the audience decided to take my picture and post it on their social media account. It was a harmless post meant to give me good press. The only problem was this amateur photographer took my picture below stage level, which created a disproportionate view of my stature. I was horrified to see myself looking like a fifty-pound overweight female because of the camera angle. It taught me to consider the angle when taking a picture, and you can bet I'm going to ask a client or friend for approval before posting their picture online. Don't lose money because of one ill-fated picture on social media!

Posting pictures of others

Always ask someone before posting and tagging a picture of them. You wouldn't want to lose a potential client or friend or give a false impression due to one misstep.

Filters and blockers aren't always bad.

Play it safe and use a filter on your social media so you can decide if you want someone's mistake to show up on your feed. In other words, utilize a filter on your social media that requires you to accept or decline a tagged picture.

Are you a story hog?

If your co-worker, friend, or relative has big news, allow them to announce it on social media before you take the liberty to do so. You could easily offend many people by beating them to the punch. Let them spread the good news and congratulate them when appropriate.

So, you have big news to announce?

On the flip side, if you are making an announcement, consider those around you and the effects it might have before posting. Are you going to offend a potential new client you've been trying to win over when you note on social media that you have started using their competition? A private conversation about your lifelong relationship with the other vendor before posting might be more palatable for the new client you are trying to win over, saving the relationship. This rule comes in handy for family and friends too. Consider having a quick conversation with close friends or family before posting about an engagement, birth, or new job.

People are always watching.

You never know who your next client, friend, or family member will be. You could cut your client base in half by posting something political, crude, or questionable.

Just scrolling through social media?

The phrase, "If you don't have anything nice to say, don't say anything" is a good rule to remember. Someone asks a question on social media about a local mom-and-pop business that you've never patronized, and you decide to reply with something negative about the location or your dislike for the style of food. The potential for looking negative, losing potential clients, and hurting a small business that you haven't frequented is great. Keep scrolling and continue to refrain from negative behavior.

Just the facts, please

If you are posting or replying to information on social media, make sure to investigate and publish the truth before emphatically stating a piece of information that may or may not be correct. For example, a store is closing; a candidate just declared winner; a restaurant only serves beef. You could be discouraging sales from these businesses and make yourself look unpolished and unprofessional by spreading false information. After all, people want to do business with those who are knowledgeable, trustworthy, and not gossipy. Would you want to do business with someone who has a reputation for spreading false information?

FROZEN IN TIME

Technology can be our best friend, and technology can also be the biggest party pooper of our lives. It interrupts our own story, interrupts our ability to have a thought or a daydream, to imagine something wonderful, because we're too busy bridging the walk from the cafeteria back to the office on the cell phone.

~ Steven Spielberg[4]

NAVIGATING THE GLACIERS

I was on a plane recently and, before take-off, a passenger in the row in front of me received a phone call. I couldn't help but be intrigued by her call; business is conducted remotely a lot these days, and it was a business call. The owner of the company answered in an irritated, huffy voice by stating her first name. As the conversation proceeded, she eventually mentioned her company name. I assumed the caller was confused with her non-business response, and the owner realized it was a potential client, because of how the conversation abruptly turned. The owner began to speak loudly, rattling off valuable information, including an address, gate code, and account number. Other passengers began to get irritated with the loud business call, and eventually, the flight attendant approached the woman, asking her to turn off her phone in preparation for takeoff. I had heard of her company but immediately decided I would never do business with her. The rude behavior, lack of courtesy for others on the plane, and evidence of secure information being leaked gave me great cause for concern. I wonder how many other future clients she lost that day due to her behavior. The irony is that she was the owner of a security company. I can assure you she didn't get my business, resulting in a loss of money for her!

Answering for business

Whether you are in a brick-and-mortar business or conducting business remotely, answer the phone stating your name and business. You want to establish confidence with future clients and sound professional at the same time. You run the risk of sounding like a novice or start-up if you answer with only a hello.

What is your countenance when answering?

Practice smiling when answering the phone. It sounds crazy, but smiling while answering the phone can make you sound happier and more upbeat. Who wants to call a business that sounds grouchy?

How are others hearing you?

So many times, the person answering a business phone makes the first impression with possible clients. Record yourself or the staff talking on the phone and listen to the tone of voice. Is it cheery or depressing? Practice enunciating clearly and speaking slowly enough that your name and company name can be easily under-

stood. You want to make a positive impression so your company is remembered for future business.

How confident do you sound?

A client calls and asks if your business sells a certain service or product. How you respond can build confidence or scare people away. For example, someone calls and asks if you sell a certain product and you answer, "I think so" with a tone that suggests you are unsure. You've just put a question mark in your future client's mind, encouraging them to check elsewhere.

Are you huffy and choppy?

When you have had a bad day, try to not convey it to your caller. A choppy, short answer or a huffy sigh (coming across like I can't believe you would bother me with a question like that) can easily turn away any caller.

How are you conveying information?

You answer and the caller wants information. Speak slowly and enunciate clearly, especially if you are giving an address, email address, or phone number. It never hurts to repeat the information or break it down—E as in echo, B as in bravo, etc.

How are you remembering?

Paper, phones, computers, iPads, and other creative sources are at everyone's fingertips. Take notes so you can easily remember important and casual information to continue building confidence with your clients and business associates. Having to call someone back several times because you didn't take notes can look bad.

Have you thought about volume?

Are you naturally a loud talker or a whisperer? Loud talkers should be careful to not talk so people across the room can hear every phone conversation, accidentally giving out personal information or irritating others. On the flip side, if you are normally a whisperer, speak up so people can hear you. You wouldn't want to lose business because someone couldn't hear you when giving out a name, phone number, website, or other important pieces of information.

When to use a speaker phone

We've all been in a place where someone pulls out their phone to talk and immediately turns it on speaker for all to hear. Remember to use speaker phone only if you are by yourself or on a planned group call. It's hard to win trust and favor with people you are irritating or potentially giving out someone else's personal information. If you have a hard time hearing, step away into a more private area to talk.

What about receiving a call in a car while traveling with others?

Unless it is time-sensitive or urgent, let the call go to voicemail, showing common courtesy to those in the vehicle with you. If you must answer, excuse yourself and talk quietly and make the conversation short, not irritating those around you.

What about voicemail?

This subject runs the gamut with people of all ages. If you are running a business, check voicemail periodically, even if you don't like to use it. Some prefer to leave a message but others don't. Get in the habit of checking your phone to head off unclear communication or disastrous business trauma. Listening to voicemails in the car while driving home alone, or creating a designated time to check, is a good idea. It's also easy these days to read your voicemail on most phones, speeding up the process.

Are you multitasking?

When taking a business call, give the caller your undivided attention. Talking to someone on the phone and suddenly stopping to talk to another person at the same time is a great way to turn off clients. For example, "Mr. Jones, we have a proposal for you... Marge get me a diet coke when you come back this way..."

Several calls at once?

If you are juggling several calls at once, politely (with a cheery voice) ask to put them on hold and wait for their consent. Don't say, "Hold" and immediately click over to the next person. You want to ensure the potential client is still holding when you return to them.

Professional versus personal

When conducting business and in doubt, use formal titles like Mr. or Mrs. and steer clear of foul language. There is a big difference between professional and personal calls. A personal call may allow you to call someone by their nickname and joke accordingly.

Call merging

You may be in a situation where you need to merge a caller with a stranger. Remember to politely ask the first person to hold while you merge, and when connected, introduce the two parties to eliminate any awkwardness. It's much easier to talk to a new person if you can call them by name rather than caller number three.

Time to call

Consider the person you are calling. Try not to call before 8:00 am (typical business start time) or later than 9:00 pm.

What to do with your phone during a meeting

Keep your phone in your lap, handbag, or pocket during a meeting. Placing your phone on the table signals to your boss, client, or presenter that the phone call you may be getting is more important than they are.

Can you hear me?

Show courtesy when placing a call to make sure the recipient can easily hear you. This might involve making sure you aren't in a noisy place or not on speakerphone with someone hard of hearing.

Lost reception

If you have a dropped call don't make accusations like, "Your phone disconnected us," or "What did you do to drop our call?" Just call back, acknowledge the disruption, and continue your conversation.

Placing a call

Introduce yourself with your first and last name and remind the person you are calling who you are if you've met previously. This will jog their memory and keep them from having to guess who you are.

Courtesy with time

If calling someone with a lengthy topic, ask if it is a good time to talk. After making quick pleasantries, get to business, and be respectful of their time.

Oh, did you want to talk?

Give the other person time to talk and make sure to not dominate the conversation.

Returning a call

If someone left you a message, stick to the twenty-four-hour rule and call back within that timeframe. If you can't return the call immediately, set a timer, text yourself, or write a note to remind yourself to return the call. Not returning a call is a great way to lose business.

You've accidentally overlooked a phone call

Apologize to the caller and make a mental note to check your call log often so you don't overlook any other calls. Not returning a call from a potential client could ultimately drive them away.

Ending a call

If trying to earn trust and favor, end the call with a pleasant tone and don't sound rushed when disconnecting.

Landline or cell phone

Remember that a landline may not show your phone number, so leave your number if you want someone to call you back.

<u>Text Messaging</u>

FROZEN IN TIME
When I'm texting you, you should know that I'm smiling.
- Unknown

NAVIGATING THE GLACIERS

Phones have changed our world in so many ways. Not that long ago, we had one phone on the wall with a long stretchy cord. Today, most people around the globe have their own handheld device, which can do so much good or harm. During my days as a physician coach, I watched patients pour out their major health concerns to their trusted doctor only to be offended when they watched the doctor grab a cell phone and begin to type. Most of the time the doctor was trying to look up needed information to convey to the patient. It was never explained to the patient, and the patient was typically offended, thinking the doctor had more important things to do than listen to the patient's situation. This crisis can be easily remedied. Don't let your phone get between you and a current or potential client, resulting in a loss of money or positive relationships.

What is your texting saying to those around you?

If you want to look up a piece of information while in a conversation with others, politely acknowledge what you are doing so they don't think you are being rude and checking out.

Are you texting in front of others?

Randomly picking up your phone to text while in the middle of a conversation can give a bad impression, indicating that your text is more important than the current conversation. If it's time-sensitive, excuse yourself but reengage quickly; otherwise, let the text wait.

When not to text

If you are giving bad news like a breakup, loss of job, or death of a friend, attempt to talk in person. At the very least, make a phone call so the recipient can hear your tone of voice and isn't shocked by a text.

What to do after receiving a text?

Acknowledge you have received a text, especially in business, so you aren't keeping the other person waiting on pins and needles.

Texting someone you don't normally communicate with

Make sure to include your name when texting with those you don't normally text with. You are showing common courtesy by reminding them of your name. And this is helpful in case you aren't in their phone directory. You might even receive a return text if the recipient knows it's not a scammer.

Keeping your texting brief

If your text is long, consider emailing the recipient instead for ease of reading, but you can text letting them know you just sent an email.

Personal or confidential

Remember that people can accidentally read someone's phone, and screenshots are easy to take, so confidential information may become public if you text it.

Texting in a play, church, or movie

Your phone light can disturb those around you. If you have to text, pick an appropriate time to slip out and text.

You receive an important text but need to reply later.

After you've received a text and acknowledged receipt, pin the text at the top of your phone to make it easy to find and serve as a quick reminder to reply later.

How much time do you have to reply to a text?

A text is more casual than a phone call, so set a couple of times in your daily schedule to return all texts.

What about autocorrect?

This feature can be wonderful, but it can also be terrifying! Get into the habit of proofing your text before hitting send. You won't come across as a competent businessperson or reliable individual if you are constantly sending texts with typos or inaccurate wording.

Read the text thread.

If you want to appear confident and knowledgeable, scroll through the previous text thread to make sure you don't already have the information in hand. This shows courtesy and competence.

Abbreviations

Not everyone is familiar with popular abbreviations, so if in doubt... u should spl out the word, k!

Zoom, Google Chat, and FaceTime

FROZEN IN TIME

Remember that the Zoom room isn't magical and you need to prepare and help yourself to create the conditions for focus.
- Terri Francis

NAVIGATING THE GLACIERS

Zoom, Google Chat, and other video communication picked up due to the pandemic and created many social dilemmas. I have engaged in many Zoom meetings and have witnessed numerous funny events simply because people weren't aware of Zoom procedures. During the height of the pandemic, when people were conducting business primarily online, I was in a Zoom meeting with other individuals. During the call, I was distracted by one businessman who hadn't taken the time to prepare the background or himself for the meeting. He had a junky background with stacks of papers, trash, boxes, bags, and random items that wouldn't normally be seen in a professional office. He happened to be a financial advisor, and the Zoom meeting consisted of others who might need his services or could give him a good referral. The unorganized background immediately made me wonder how he would handle my financial affairs. I was still feeling somewhat positive about him, giving him grace for his messy office, but when he stood to retrieve an important document, he revealed that he wasn't dressed from head to toe in business attire. He had on a dress shirt, tie, and blazer but chose not to wear the matching dress pants. We all laughed, and I immediately began to question his everyday business savviness. Long story short, he lost several potential clients that day simply because of his business presentation.

Find the mute button.

When on a Zoom call and someone is presenting, make sure to mute yourself so your background noise, coughing, chair movement, or other noises don't become a distraction. Not muting is the email equivalent of reply all.

Ready to talk?

Be positioned with the mute button before you start to speak so that you appear knowledgeable and show courtesy with everyone's time.

Are you a distraction?

When involved with a Zoom call, keep your movements to a minimum. Moving papers, playing with your hair, eating, and changing sitting positions can all become a distraction to others on the call.

Moving while Zooming?

If you must be on a Zoom call while moving or walking around your office or house, make sure to mute the call to eliminate background noise, and turn off video to lessen distractions.

Does this make me look fat?

Notice the angle of the phone or computer. A computer angled upward could give you a double chin or exaggerated nose if not positioned carefully.

What about the background?

If you are trying to appear professional, make sure your background shows it. A messy office or untidy house could turn off potential clients on a Zoom call. Some might equate a messy office or scattered belongings with a lower level of service.

Consider the lighting.

Use a well-lit room, window seat, or attachable light when on a Zoom call so others can see you, and you come across as trustworthy. Sitting in a dark room while conducting business may come across as questionable and can be unflattering.

FROZEN IN TIME

Sometimes you have to disconnect to stay connected. Remember the old days when you had eye contact during a conversation? When everyone wasn't looking down at a device in their hands? We've become so focused on that tiny screen that we forget the big picture, the people right in front of us.
~ Regina Brett

NAVIGATING THE GLACIERS

While sitting in a local coffee shop writing this book, a couple of ladies with a young boy walked in. The ladies ordered their coffee and a large chocolate chip cookie for the boy and immediately began a lively conversation. The young boy was left to entertain himself while the ladies talked excitedly. Within seconds, he took out his iPad and began to play a game. Unaware of the loud game noises, which drowned out the soothing music being played in the coffee shop, the ladies talked loudly. The high-pitched, quick-tempo game quickly became a distraction to those studying, reading, or having conversations with friends.

I understood the mom wanted her young child to be distracted while she talked with her friend, but she didn't seem to consider others and how they might be disturbed by the gaming noise. The ladies could have chosen an area in the corner away from other people, or the mom and/or her child could have muted the game. Either of those options would have alleviated staff concerns about the comfort of other patrons, and the calm vibe in the coffee shop would have gone undisturbed. As it was, the child was entertained while the ladies babbled on, unaware of their surroundings.

For adults, the use of a phone at a business lunch is acceptable only if the user lets the other person know that they may be receiving a business call. A cell phone during dinner is not acceptable. This is a great lesson to teach children so they understand how their phone or device can alienate others or come across as rude.

In a restaurant with children and you have a cell phone/mobile device dilemma.

Sitting at a table in a restaurant while waiting for food can be used as a learning opportunity for children. This is a great time for an adult to model verbal skills and table manners, and ask a few indirect questions that might give insight into what a child might be thinking. It is also a good time to incorporate a quick game involving hidden math or English skills instead of allowing your child to drown themselves in a game while waiting on food.

<u>Written Word</u>

A handwritten thank you note shows the giver that you, as the receiver, have taken the time to express gratitude for a gift or sacrifice, and it warms the heart of the giver. This is a two-way process, which perpetuates generosity and thankfulness. Although not the intent of gratitude, receiving appreciation often perpetuates further generosity. A continued spirit of thankfulness and generosity is something our society could improve upon.

FROZEN IN TIME

We must find time to stop and thank the people who make a
difference in our lives.
~ John F. Kennedy

In 1864 Lincoln received a gift from one of his generals. Sherman sent a message, "I beg to present to you as a Christmas gift the City of Savannah, with one hundred and fifty guns and plenty of ammunition, also about twenty-five thousand bales of cotton." Four days later Lincoln sent a thank you note, "Many, many thanks for your Christmas gift —the capture of Savannah."[5]

NAVIGATING THE GLACIERS

After receiving a business gift, being the recipient of a surprise office party, or attending other events where gifts are received, it may seem like a chore to write individual notes of thanks to everyone. But if Lincoln, who came from the backwoods of Tennessee, took the time to say thanks, it might behoove us to learn from his example regardless of the value of the gift. The use of a handwritten note can set your business apart from others; this one act goes a long way in differentiating your business. A handwritten note may create a positive first impression or reinforce client trust. Once you've learned these rules of etiquette, you will notice the difference when you are working with others who don't. Knowledge is power, especially in this area.

Keep your clients and earn their respect and money by simply utilizing manners and writing a thank you note.

Handwritten thank-you

It is always appropriate to express gratitude, especially in a handwritten format. A handwritten note shows you've gone the extra mile to show appreciation.

Timeline for writing a thank you note

Write the note as soon as possible, and remember it's never too late to write a note if you've been delayed.

Body of the note

If your gift came from a couple, make sure you acknowledge both people when saying thank you. The person who purchased, packaged, and mailed your gift might have been the spouse, and if you only thank one-half of the couple, you could be offending the one who went to all the effort to gift you.

Personalize it.

When writing a thank you note, thank the person for the gift, even if you didn't like it. Stay away from generalized comments and say something specific about the gift: "The blue dish will look great in my new kitchen." This shows you have taken the time to recognize the gift that was given, and you aren't sending out mass thank you notes. Use your creativity and heartfelt thoughts. It's okay to keep it brief.

Addressing your note

Take time to look up the proper spelling of someone's name. It's easy these days to find the correct spelling and rather embarrassing if you address a note to a good friend and misspell their name. For example, check to see if Ronny is spelled with an "ie" or "y."

Using a title

Always use the proper title for an individual in a formal or business occasion. Using the title of Doctor, Honorable, or Colonel are appropriate for a wedding or graduation as well as business communication. Electronic sources can be your best friend if you don't know someone's title. Always err on the side of being correct and formal if in doubt.

Directions

Make sure you stuff the envelope correctly after you've written your note. When placing the note inside the envelope, turn the envelope over so the back side is facing you, turn your written note facing you, and slide the note into the envelope so when the recipient opens the card, they can slide the card out facing up.

Email With Style

There are differing views on email etiquette. Take a look at, brush up on, and utilize email etiquette to avoid losing a client or financial transaction due to a poorly-written email.

FROZEN IN TIME

*Everybody gets so much information all day long
that they lose their common sense.*
~ Gertrude Stein

NAVIGATING GLACIER MOMENTS

Have you ever had a typo in an email? I recently had someone email me while accidentally copying another person on the same email. This other person wasn't privy to the information being spelled out in the email, thus creating a negative situation because the person writing the email didn't proofread it. Needless to say, the vendor lost out on money because of his careless mistake, which happened to be the final straw in a long line of other careless mistakes.

Subject line

Choose your subject line carefully. This can be helpful for both you and your client for immediate deciphering and easy retrieval if necessary.

All Caps

All caps should be avoided; it may sound angry. Remember, you are gaining client trust, and shouting may not get the job done.

Humor

Remember that humor doesn't always translate well to other people or different cultures. What you think is funny may be insulting to others. Sarcasm, double entendre, and time-sensitive quotes are great examples of items that should be avoided.

Proofread

Proofreading is a must! If you find yourself lacking in this area, call a business associate for help. This one rule of etiquette could help you avoid losing a client. Do your best to catch a misplaced comma, misspelled name, or accidental innuendo.

If you have accidentally made a *faux pas* with texting, emailing, or written cards, you understand the emotional impact you can inadvertently make. This is the perfect segue to the last topic of this book regarding this three-step method to turn your manners into money. ICE, which consists of Impression, Communication, and Empathy also involves emotion.

*Money, like emotions, is something you must control
to keep your life on the right track.*
- Natasha Munson.

APPLY ICE

<u>Preparing for a Name Encounter</u>

If you are attending an event and anticipate running into people you may not remember, enlist a friend or colleague to step up and introduce themselves first, prompting that person to say their name aloud so you can be reminded of their name.

Here are some other communication tips to keep in mind:

- Create a plan with a coworker, friend, or spouse on how to handle forgetting someone's name.
- Keep up with new terminology for different age groups, including abbreviations, memes, and gifs.
- Practice utilizing soothing words instead of absolutes or words that stir up controversy.
- Type the body of your email first, proofread it, and then type in the person's email address to avoid accidentally sending an email with potential mistakes.
- Look up the spelling of someone's name (Facebook and LinkedIn are great resources) before texting, writing, emailing, or using social media.
- Utilize the talents of a person who is good with details before a Zoom call to make sure background items don't become an issue and end up losing you money.

Chapter Four

EMPATHY

TURN MANNER$ INTO MONEY WITHOUT BEING COLD AS ICE

FROZEN IN TIME

Empathy is seeing with the eyes of another, listening with the ears of another, and feeling with the heart of another.
- Alfred Adler

Awareness of others and assessing the situation is a key component when utilizing manners. Manners are used to make other people feel comfortable and earn their trust. Knowing or understanding a situation is key when knowing which manners to utilize to make the correct response.

NAVIGATING GLACIER MOMENTS

In one of my coaching sessions assisting a medical provider to increase his patient satisfaction scores, I witnessed an encounter that didn't end well but could have been avoided. One patient was a sweet, older lady dressed in comfortable but classy dress shoes, wrapped in a beautiful plaid sweater over an untucked blouse with stylish slacks. She had carefully styled gray hair, and her cell phone had pictures of her grandchildren as the background. After the medical provider systematically stated the medications he was providing and the instructions on how to take them, he stood, said goodbye, and quickly left the exam room.

I noticed a grimace and a confused look on the patient's face as she gathered her belongings and left. She mumbled under her breath that the doctor was unkind and didn't spend enough time with her. It was evident that the situation could have been avoided if the doctor had taken the time to notice she was a loving grandmother, remarked about her beautiful grandkids, and given medical instructions in a warm, loving manner. Noticing and expressing empathy is key in utilizing manners in an appropriate way to relate to people in different business situations and stay on top of your business and financial goals.

When trying to make a great first impression or trying to make people feel comfortable, little things make all the difference in the world. If you are trying to impress a new client or possible boss, manners (even if the other person isn't well-trained in them) can make or break a situation because it is all about making that person feel important and respected.

FROZEN IN TIME

Life is like an elevator. Up and down, just make sure you get off on the right floor.
- Keith Douglas

NAVIGATING GLACIER MOMENTS

I worked in a high-rise building in one of my first jobs out of college. I had never been particularly fond of elevators, but my job entailed riding them to and from the parking garage and to other floors when delivering items to different businesses. One day, I jumped on the elevator to hand deliver some paperwork to a vendor when a gentleman entered the elevator after me. We began our ascent to a higher floor but the elevator came to a sudden halt, jarring us as we wondered what was happening. I felt the hair on the back of my neck stand to attention and my blood pressure spike as I realized I was trapped in an elevator with a strange man.

After several failed attempts at using the elevator phone, we tried to think of an escape plan. We tried to pry the elevator doors open, but it only allowed us to open the doors less than an inch. We realized we were trapped between floors and could barely make out a receptionist on an upper floor. We yelled, hit the doors, and stuck paper through the door to get the receptionist's attention. We ended up being stuck in the elevator for about an hour.

Many elevator rules of etiquette were broken that day, which can be learned about in the following section. The vendor didn't receive any more of our business due to their less than courteous attitude.. I eventually had to climb out with the help of a fireman. Because the man on the elevator refrained from helping me, he didn't earn any respect or business from me. The vendor, upon receiving the paperwork I had set out to deliver, barely uttered an audible thank you, even after hearing about my trauma. That incident gave me a new appreciation for elevator etiquette, and I hope it will give you some insight the next time you ride.

Who goes first?

When waiting to get on an elevator and the door opens, stand aside to allow the people on the elevator to exit first. This courtesy makes common sense, allowing the elevator to empty before filling up again and preventing a jam.

Button, button, who's got the button?

If you are on the elevator, standing close to the control panel (buttons), politely ask what floor is needed by everyone and push the buttons for them. This prevents people from awkwardly crowding the panel, and you are showing care for the other riders.

Positions, please

If riding an elevator with strangers, providing personal space and facing forward can easily make individuals feel more at ease.

Acknowledgment

A quick hello, good morning, or good evening provides a comfortable ice breaker and, who knows, you might make a quick connection and gain a new client with your brief encounter.

Luggage cart

If you are trying to get on an elevator with a luggage cart but the elevator has passengers, either wait for the next elevator or proceed if the riders invite you on. It's better to wait for an empty elevator than make everyone on board feel uncomfortable and cramped.

Stand or pivot

If you are standing in the front of an elevator with just a few riders but aren't exiting when the doors open, politely stand aside or pivot and let those in the back exit quickly. You can also step out of the elevator, hold the door open while other passengers exit, then return to your spot in the elevator.

What about capacity?

Riding on an elevator is a stress-free event for some and a tense situation for others. If you are in a semi-crowded elevator and the doors open with others wanting to enter, be cognizant of those already on board. A simple statement, "We will send the elevator back after we've emptied it" will suffice.

Juicy conversation

You are in the middle of a juicy conversation, and the elevator arrives at its desired location. Politely pause your story, step off quickly, or allow those who need to exit to leave, then continue your story. Instead of causing others to stand and listen to your ending comments, have their work schedule held up, or increase their claustrophobic stress, delay your conversation.

Elevator chit chat

Quick, polite greetings are appropriate, but keep personal conversations to a minimum with other riders on board, especially if you are using strong or questionable language with small children present.

<u>Escalator & Moving Sidewalks</u>

FROZEN IN TIME

Let us be like an escalator...lifting others up with power...step lifting them even without power.
- VSon

NAVIGATING THE GLACIERS

Most of us have been in an airport, navigating around people on an escalator or moving sidewalk. A few years ago, my husband and I were in a different country, and our plane was delayed. We found ourselves rushing to make our connecting flight. It was in a different terminal, and we had minutes to make our way through the crowded airport to our airplane. Knowing it would be an ordeal if we missed our plane, we would do whatever it took to catch that last flight. In our journey across the airport, we had to navigate both escalators and moving sidewalks. I quickly realized why the rules of etiquette in that situation were so important. If you've ever tried to use an escalator or moving sidewalk and encountered people who were completely oblivious to these rules (sprawled out, leaving no room for panicked travelers), you will understand the need for escalator etiquette.

Start the ascent.

Step onto the escalator and carefully grab the rail if needed. It is easier to steady yourself than create a traffic jam by stumbling and falling.

Who goes first?

Whether going up or down, when stepping onto an escalator, the female should precede the male, protecting the female in case she stumbles backward.

Side rails

If your hands are dirty, try to minimize exposure so you don't contaminate other riders. Covid has made everyone aware of this courtesy.

Emergency stop

> *Make yourself aware of the emergency stop button in case it is needed.*

Right or left?

> *When riding an escalator or moving sidewalk, stand to the right so people wanting to pass can move by quickly.*

What about the arms?

> *When riding an escalator, think about those passing on the left. Hang onto the right side so others can pass if necessary.*

Grocery Stores, Hallways & Common Areas

FROZEN IN TIME

I like being able to go grocery shopping and not feel that I'm fighting a thousand people.
~ Roz Chast

NAVIGATING THE GLACIERS

Going to the grocery store is sometimes a quick event and other times a long endeavor. Politeness is always in style, but it often seems forgotten in the aisles of grocery stores. On one occasion, I vividly remember making a mad dash to the store to get some items for an impromptu dinner party that was to take place at our house later in the evening. With a grocery list in hand and limited time, I began to make my way up and down the isles but still wanted to practice good manners while shopping. I noticed my time slipping away, and I had one more item to purchase before running home to prepare the meal. As I stood looking intently for that one obscure item, I saw someone approach as if needing to make their way to items on the other end of the shelves. I naturally stepped back to let them pass, which is common courtesy, and was surprised and frustrated when the shopper stopped and stood between me and the shelves I was studying. Being aware of others, not blocking people, and showing courtesy goes a long way in making the dreadful chore of grocery shopping a little more palatable. And it can prevent issues and harsh conversations among people.

By the way, the meal turned out fine, I was just a little late putting it in the oven after my delay at the store. What I didn't realize was that someone from my business circle was watching to see how I handled the situation. Thank goodness I was behaving myself that day and responded appropriately. A gentle response and a little extra patience paid off, and I didn't realize it until the observer told me a few days later after the grocery store event.

Driving rules

Think about walking the grocery store aisles like you would the roads of town. When you come to the end of the aisle, look both ways before darting out.

Stopping in the middle of the aisle

If you need to stop to look at items on the shelf, push your basket to one side instead of leaving it out in the middle so others can pass by easily.

Time to check your grocery list

If you need to check your grocery list, pull your basket to the side or into an empty aisle before making a stop to check your list.

Conversations with friends

Chances are great you will eventually run into someone you know at the store. Exchange greetings then move to the side for other shoppers to pass. Use situational awareness so you don't hold up others around you.

Walking side by side

Be cognizant of other shoppers if you are walking side by side down an aisle. When you hear or see someone approaching, move to the side to let them pass easily.

Shopping slowly

Shop at your own pace but remain cognizant of those around you and let them pass. If someone wants to look at the same item, offer to share the space or let them collect their item and you go back to shopping.

Passing other shoppers

Situational awareness and positioning of your shopping cart are important. If you see someone who has stopped to shop and you are pushing a basket, walk past them with your basket not blocking the other shopper from shopping view.

Getting to the item you need

In a polite tone of voice with neutral body language, plainly say, "Excuse me," select your item, and move on. Make sure you are speaking in an appropriate volume with a courteous tone, modeling great manners.

Cell phone talkers with speakers

If speaking with someone on your cell phone, refrain from using speaker phone. Other shoppers don't need to hear about Aunt Mildred and her bursitis, and I don't think Aunt Mildred would be happy if others knew all her details either.

Cell phone talkers and volume

People tend to speak louder when talking on the phone, so if you are in a store and you must talk, speak at a lower volume.

Checking out

Personal space is important when checking out. Allow the person in front of you to put their items on the conveyor belt and give them at least a foot of space before placing your items. This was a

*pre-pandemic concept and still exists today, but is more under-
standable now.*

Grocery cart storage

*Model great manners by returning your cart to the designated cart
return. You wouldn't want to be guilty of allowing your stray cart
to hit a vehicle or person. There are cameras everywhere these
days, and chances are great you would be easy to track down if you
were guilty of your rolling cart running into a person or someone's
car.*

Are You a Good Neighbor?

Neighbors can make life enjoyable or miserable, depending
on how we interact with them. There is an art to developing
great relationships with people who live nearby, and if
handled correctly, may even become some of your greatest
clients and friends.

FROZEN IN TIME

A good neighbor—a found treasure.
- Chinese Proverb

NAVIGATING THE GLACIERS

Great neighbors are a fantastic find and can make life more enjoyable, but many things can happen to ruin that special relationship. Great neighbors might end up being the ones you call for an emergency recipe ingredient, help when needing a second set of hands, or keep an eye on your house when traveling. One time when we were on a trip, the electricity went out, and our neighbors called to let us know. They went into the house and took care of melting ice from the freezer.

Walking your dog

Carry a disposable bag to collect unwanted doggie deposits and retain good neighbor relationships.

Barking dog?

Remain vigilant about keeping your dog's barking to a minimum, especially late at night or early in the morning.

Planning a big party

Give your neighbors a heads-up that there will be extra cars on the street. When appropriate, invite them to the party too. It's hard for neighbors to complain if they are at your house enjoying themselves with you!

Mailboxes

Make sure you aren't blocking a neighbor's mailbox with your car or your guest's car.

No HOA?

Chances are great that if you have an HOA, you are abiding by neighborhood rules. But if you don't have an HOA, make it your goal to make sure you don't have the most unkempt house in the neighborhood with tall grass, overdue edging needs, junky decorations, or obvious poor house maintenance.

Welcoming new neighbors

Just like the Chinese Proverb says, a good neighbor is a found treasure. Create great relationships by remembering your current neighbors and welcoming new neighbors with a plate of cookies or sweets. In other words, thinking of others around you is one of the ultimate things that can be exemplified using great manners.

Communication with neighbors

Politeness with your neighbors may involve a friendly wave whenever passing in the neighborhood to an occasional front porch chat.

Don't take advantage

*People of different occupations and talents reside in your neighbor-
hood and are good to have around. Use caution when calling on
them so you don't take advantage of their expertise.*

Trash Day

*Remain respectful of your neighbors on trash pickup days, espe-
cially if your trash is blowing into other yards. Be that great
neighbor who goes the extra mile by taking in your neighbor's
trashcan when they are gone or out late.*

Respect for personal property

*Don't assume it's okay to enter your neighbor's backyard to retrieve
a ball or some other object without permission.*

Before and after-hours yard work

*If you like to do yard work, respect neighbors by limiting mowing
and other loud chores to waking hours, not before 7:00 am on a
Saturday or after 10:00 pm.*

<u>The Gift That Keeps on Giving</u>

Giving gifts, large or small, can make a big impact; but if
not done properly, can put a bad taste in someone's mouth
and create a negative relationship.

FROZEN IN TIME

The meaning of life is to find your gift. The purpose of life is to give it away.
~ Pablo Picasso

NAVIGATING THE GLACIERS

Our second child promptly arrived on her due date, weighing 10 pounds 6 ounces, with a full head of hair and two teeth. As a new mom, I was excited to receive baby gifts, including clothes to adorn our new baby girl. One day, a sweet senior lady presented me with a cute pink dress for my baby girl. As I eagerly opened the box, I folded back the tissue paper to reveal a pink preemie-sized dress with white lace. There was a garage sale sticker that said twenty-five cents. My little bundle of joy wasn't going to fit in the dress, and I was taken aback that it had been purchased at a garage sale. I know the shock on my face was evident, but when I looked into the eyes of the older lady, I quickly realized she was thrilled with her gift. It was at that point I was reminded that it's about the giver, not the gift. This lady had gone out of her way to shop for a gift, wrap it up, and hunt me down to give me a token of her love.

How do you respond when receiving a gift? This one act, if performed properly, could gain you a new client, resulting in more money. Or it can have the opposite effect if done incorrectly.

Reaction to a gift

Always be appreciative and respond with thankfulness when receiving a gift.

Can't or won't use the gift

Graciously receive a gift that is given to you even if you don't care for it and thank the giver; they are trying to bless you.

Showing appreciation

It is always appropriate to show appreciation for a gift, and hand-written notes are the best way to do so. It shows you have gone out of your way to say thanks.

Receiving an awful gift

You've received a horrible gift and can't find anything positive to say about it. Simply thank the giver for remembering you. Making comments like, "This is an interesting gift," or "This is unique," can easily ruin a moment and a relationship.

Hostess gift

A small gift for your host, showing your appreciation, is appropriate: flowers, a bottle of wine, or something that doesn't create more work for your host is ideal.

Opening a gift

It is fitting to open a gift in front of the giver so they can see your positive reaction, and you can thank them in the moment.

Regifting

The main thing to remember here is to not offend anyone! Regifting should be done sparingly with a few things in mind. Make sure it's not a personalized gift, and make sure the item is brand new and in the original packaging. Try limiting regifting to brand-new items that are duplicates you've received. These can be great last-minute gifts for emergencies. You don't want to create ill feelings with the person who gave you the gift or the person you are giving it to. It's always better to err on the side of caution than ruin a friendship due to laziness or inconvenience. Go the extra mile and let the receiver know you are regifting to avoid any potential ill feelings from all parties involved.

Giving to be seen

Give your gift and allow the receiver to take it from there. Don't insist on them showing everyone your gift. There may be those who can't give as large a gift, so give with the spirit of love not a bragging demeanor.

Table Manners

A good test for an employer to get to know and understand a job candidate is to take them out to a nice restaurant. At this point, it is easy to observe a person's knowledge of table manners, conversation starters with waiters, patience level with strangers, and the ability to appear calm and composed. Want to turn manners into money? Utilize great table manners so you can pass your next on-the-job interview.

FROZEN IN TIME

The world was my oyster, but I used the wrong fork.
~ Oscar Wilde

NAVIGATING THE GLACIERS

Years ago, I had a dinner engagement with a new, wealthy client. My first impression didn't go well because I inadvertently grabbed the wrong salad plate. It may seem rather innocent, but this well-educated, refined lady noticed my mistake. We laughed about it and finished our meal. The problem was I had to work twice as hard in the following months to earn her respect and eventual business. I could have made my life a little less stressful if I had taken the time to remind myself of table etiquette before I sat down with a new client. Position yourself well by knowing table manners so you can always relate to everyone and not lose any clients in the process.

<u>Getting Started & Where to Sit</u>

Position at the rectangular table

When attending dinner as a guest in someone's home, remember the end positions at the table are for the host and hostess. These positions allow the host and hostess easy access to get up and serve their guests when appropriate.

Unsure where to sit as a guest at a round table?

Simply ask your host or hostess where they prefer for you to sit if there aren't any name cards on the table.

When to sit

Always wait for your host or hostess to sit down or follow their invitation to sit before doing so.

The power seat

If you have been invited to a dinner or working interview, allow your host or hostess to take the power seat. The power seat is the position in a restaurant that allows your host or hostess to have the best view of the restaurant. It could be with their back to a wall, a corner of the restaurant, or any position where they can see most of the room. This allows your host to easily summon the wait staff and provide better service for you as the guest, protect a private conversation while being able to see approaching bystanders, and easily control a social setting for the betterment of the guest.

How to sit in a dining chair

Approach from the left and rise on the right.

Pulling out a chair for someone

This small gesture indicates you are looking out for someone and prevents smashing chairs into each other when everyone is approaching at the same time.

Seating arrangements

Seating arrangements are made by the host and hostess, and guests should not rearrange name cards. In some formal settings, the host or hostess will position the most powerful people in specific places.

What about the napkin?

Typically, upon sitting, you should unfold your napkin and place it in your lap. If in doubt, follow your host's lead.

Conversation Basics

Conversation at the table as a guest

Allow your host or hostess to guide the conversation during a meal.

Attending dinner with unfamiliar people

Introduce yourself to everyone at the table before sitting down to dine.

Side conversations

Make sure to include everyone in the conversation during mealtime. If there is a conversation hog, pick a moment during a lull in conversation and engage those who haven't had the opportunity to speak.

Dominating conversation

Allow for a variety of conversation topics so you don't exclude those who don't know about the dominant topic of conversation.

Eye contact

Practice alternating eye contact at the table to include everyone.

Interruptions

Wait for the person talking to finish before interrupting the conversation to ask for condiments or something else at the table.

Conversations

Stay away from controversial topics like sex, politics, relationships, and gory subjects.

Creating conversation

Try asking non-controversial, open-ended questions to engage everyone at the table.

Practice makes perfect.

Practice speaking to everyone at the table briefly, then pause to let others contribute and take turns entering the conversation.

Someone approaches your table to greet you.

Show courtesy by always standing when someone approaches your table to speak with you. If you're trapped in a booth, try standing halfway or at least attempt to stand This shows courtesy and warmth, which is appreciated when trying to earn client trust or retain great friendships.

<u>Table Incidentals</u>

When and where to place your napkin

It is appropriate to place your napkin in your lap immediately when sitting at a dinner table.

Where to place your napkin when finished with your meal

Your napkin is placed to the left of your plate when you are finished eating and standing to leave the table. Don't put a napkin

*on top of your plate; the food residue might soil the host's cloth
napkins.*

Leaving the table momentarily

*Place your napkin to the left of the plate and simply excuse your-
self. There is no need to announce you are going to the restroom. In
some formal settings, it may be proper to place your napkin on the
back of the chair.*

When to leave the table

*It is considered impolite to leave the table before your host or
hostess leaves. It is considered polite to wait until everyone is
finished before leaving the table.*

Blowing your nose

*Excuse yourself and step away from the table to blow your nose.
This eliminates the opportunity to sicken someone with your sound
and demonstration.*

How to cut your steak

*Make your initial cut through the middle of the steak and work
from inside out. Don't cut the entire steak at one time, otherwise,
the pieces will cool off faster and it won't be as tasty. Some believe
the initial constant cutting could be an interruption in the
conversation.*

Your steak has fat

A steak will have fat, so enjoy. If you find yourself making intricate, exaggerated cuts, and pushing fat piles to the side of your plate, you might inadvertently insult your host or hostess. Practice being discreet to not offend anyone at the table, especially the person who prepared the food.

How much food to leave on your plate

It is proper to leave at least one bite of food on your plate, otherwise, it might indicate to your host or hostess that they didn't feed you enough.

When to start eating at an intimate dinner

It is proper to wait until your host or hostess has started eating before everyone else begins. Someone may want to give a toast before the meal begins.

When to start eating at a restaurant in a large group

If you are in a restaurant and it is taking a while for the food to be served, it is proper for those who haven't been served to ask others to start eating so the food doesn't get cold.

When to start eating when attending a buffet

Since a buffet is more casual and it might take others a while to serve themselves, it is acceptable to begin eating after you've returned from the buffet.

Eating on a buffet line

It is never acceptable to eat while going through the buffet line.

Washing your hands

Wash your hands for your sake and everyone else's. If needed, excuse yourself, wash your hands, and return quickly.

Eating too slowly or too quickly

Pace your eating with everyone else at the table. This avoids an awkward stare from others as they are waiting for you to finish your meal.

You are served something you dislike.

If you aren't allergic to a food item, it is polite to at least take a bite of the food you don't like. The idea is to not insult your host or hostess. After taking one bite, and you still can't stomach the food, be discreet, move it around a little on your plate, show your good intentions, and make sure to thank your host or hostess.

Stacking your dirty dishes after eating at a restaurant

Even though it seems to go against being polite, it is better to not stack your dirty dishes for the waiter or waitress. They typically have a system of clearing dirty dishes and, in your effort of trying to help, it could slow them down in the process.

Passing food at a table

It is proper to pass food counterclockwise at a dinner party.

How to call a server to your table

Politeness is key when calling a server to your table. Catch their eye, raise your index finger, slightly wave your hand, or say, "Excuse me" to the server.

Making a request of the wait staff

Always use please and thank you. Don't bang on the table and try not to take too much of their time.

Tipping

Do your homework and become knowledgeable about tipping preferences in different occupations and cultures, especially when traveling abroad. Ask about tipping protocols in advance, and, above all, be respectful to wait staff. Tipping is something that is done discreetly, not making a show of the tip amount.

How much is enough?

Tipping is a way of saying thank you and subsidizes a server's income. If you can't tip, consider staying home. Consider the different trying personalities a server encounters, demonstrate grace, and tip a minimum of 15-20%. A gracious tipper is appreciated, and your generosity speaks volumes to so many people.

Proper Place Settings

Proper table settings were created in ancient times and are still observed today. As a host or hostess, you are exhibiting graciousness and appreciation to your guests who are trained in etiquette. There are casual to formal table settings, and learning the proper placement and order of items speaks volumes, especially if you are in a working interview, in the earning respect stage, or showing love when eating with family. Proper place setting creates a comfortable space for your diners, even if they aren't trained in table manners. If they are trained in proper manners, it is a win-win for everyone involved because you are creating a nonconfrontational setting, showing appreciation, and indicating that you are knowledgeable in this area. The idea is to create a comfortable space to make your guests feel well taken care of. Knowing the history and reasons for table manners gives insight and helps you remember how to create a welcoming atmosphere for your clients, friends, family, or neighbors. Keep in mind that the table setting was originally designed for right-handed people since they are in the majority.

Silverware

The amount of silverware used depends on the type of meal being served, casual versus formal, and the specific foods being served. The rule of thumb is to begin the meal using the silver on the outside and work inward.

The knife

The knife goes to the right of the plate with the blade facing the plate, otherwise it appears unfriendly and unsafe. Most people are right-handed, which is why the knife and spoon are placed on the right.

"In 1669, Louis XIV of France decreed that knives must be rounded at the top, not threateningly pointed. (Oh, wait, that was to stop people from using their knives to pick their teeth.)"[1]

Butter knife

The butter knife is the only knife that is placed to the left of the plate with the blade facing out. It is placed on the left since most people are righthanded, making it easier to grab the knife and butter to the left of the plate. If it were placed on the right side of the plate, it might cause the person doing the spreading to bump into the person sitting next to them. The butter knife has a notch at the top, which allows the bread to be spread easily. If everyone at the table is sharing a butter plate and butter knife, simply take a pat of butter, return the utensils to the plate, and pass them to the next person on your right.

The fork

It was introduced to assist when using the knife to cut food, thus the reason for being placed on the left of the plate. Usually, the only time you see a fork on the right of the plate is if you are using an oyster fork, which would be placed on the extreme right.

The spoon

The spoon is placed on the right next to the knife to be used for soup or other foods.

The napkin

As mentioned earlier, the napkin is on the left, placed in your lap upon sitting, remains in your lap throughout the meal, and left crumpled to the left of your plate when finished and leaving the table. If your silverware is rolled in a napkin, it's placed on the right because most people are right-handed.

Salt and pepper

When someone asks for the salt or pepper, always pass both at the same time. If you are at a formal table and using individualized salt and pepper containers, they should be placed above the dessert spoon; otherwise, they should be placed in the middle of the table for convenient reach of others.

Bread plate

The bread plate is to the left of your dinner plate.

Glasses

These are placed to the right of your dinner plate.

Casual place setting

A casual table setting is used in most restaurants and casual events. A casual place setting sets the tone for an informal meal and gives more room on the table without using extra silverware and utensils.

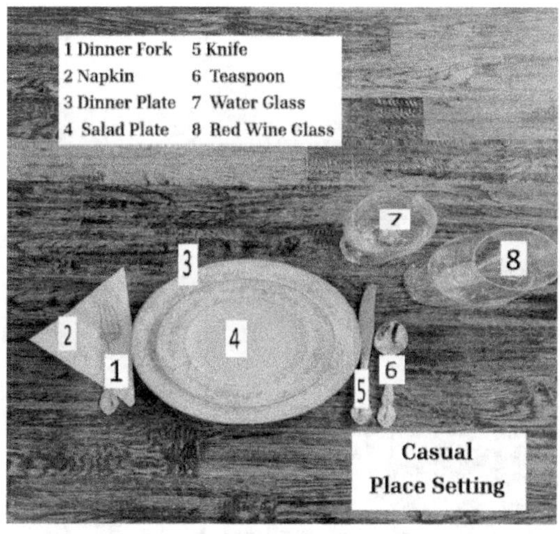

Formal place setting

A formal place setting is typically used for a black-tie event, fine restaurants, formal events, or a meal that is being served with several courses.

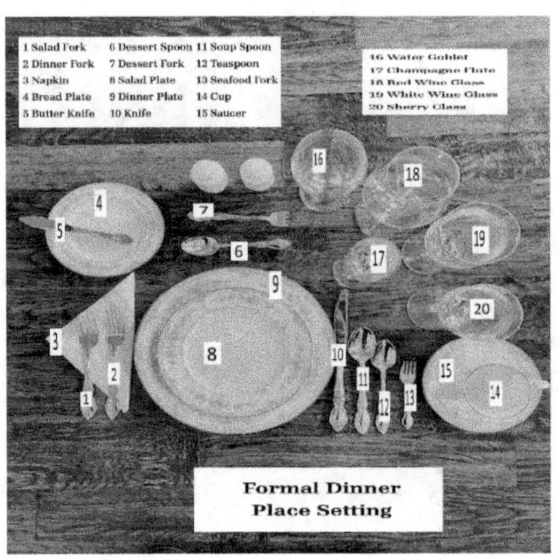

Making an Exit

FROZEN IN TIME

First impressions are important, but the last impression we leave the customer will leave the most lasting impression.
~ Shep Hyken

NAVIGATING THE GLACIERS

A few years ago, I had a visit with a local doctor whom I liked. After the visit, the medical assistant showed me the way to the check-out so that I could pay my deductible and schedule a follow-up visit. I waited patiently in the check-out chair to take care of business. The lady behind the desk turned abruptly and, in a huff as if I was disturbing her afternoon break, asked in a curt tone, "What do you need, Honey?" The hair on the back of my neck stood up when she called me "Honey." I was twice her age and didn't appreciate her condescending tone. She buried her eyes into the computer screen and never made eye contact with me again. She mumbled a few things under her breath before announcing my charge amount, birthdate, and address rather loudly so that others around could hear. She also announced I had given her the wrong insurance information and that the visit wasn't covered.

After conversing with her for a few minutes, she found the correct information (she had it all along) and stated that I only owed $20. She stated that she had to go to lunch, and I should call back to set up my follow-up visit as instructed by the doctor. She never apologized for her clerical error or huffy tone. Even though the doctor was great, this lasting impression of the check-out clerk didn't leave a good taste in my mouth, and I encountered other patients later who expressed the same sentiment.

As I left the office building, I met the parking attendant who was rude, slow to finalize my parking transaction, and never once looked me in the eye. I loved the doctor, but the lasting impressions with the check-out clerk and parking attendant caused me to think twice about seeing that doctor again. When I heard positive things about another doctor who was closer to my house, I decided to check him out and see what kind of impression he made.

Leaving a conversation, party, appointment, or meeting can either be the sweet icing on the cake or a sour dill pickle impression. It is important to leave a setting with a positive impression to gain support, continue positive relationships, and leave people wanting to come back for more. Try practicing your manners from beginning to end, and make sure you turn your manners into money with positive relationships.

Saying goodbye after a meeting or appointment

The lasting impression is vital to gaining clients and expressing appreciation of friendship to those close to you. This can be done easily by shaking hands, looking the person in the eye, smiling, and expressing a simple thank you and that you look forward to seeing them again.

Ending an appointment or meeting

If you are saying goodbye to a client or patient in your office, leave a good impression by walking them to the designated exit or checkout (or get a staff member to do it). Don't point to the end of the hall and walk away.

Goodbye conversation

Keep the goodbye brief and to the point. This isn't a time to stand around and talk about incidental things, especially if you are at a party and the host has other guests to attend.

Thank you and goodbyes at a party

If you are leaving a party, make sure to thank the host and hostess and those standing around in your immediate vicinity. It isn't necessary to draw attention to yourself in a large group by thanking everyone.

Ending a call

It may be a little trickier to end a call on a positive note, but it can be done. Leave that client or friend with a positive touch by saying thank you, slowing your speaking tempo, and making an effort to create a positive tone when saying goodbye. Practice smiling when talking on the phone. It sounds crazy, but your tone of voice comes across as more pleasant when you are smiling, even if others can't see it.

A great office visual

If you are a business owner, make sure your checkout or exit area is clean, smells pleasant, and leaves a positive sense for your clients. Is your area clean of junk, is there tasteful artwork on the walls, is the exiting door clean, and does your checkout person smile and have a warm demeanor?

A personal visual

Think about the lasting impression you are leaving people when you stand to say goodbye. Have you dressed appropriately (without any stains, wrinkles, or rips)? Are you standing with confidence (back straight, shoulders not rolled forward)? Are you looking the person in the eye? Do you have a pleasant demeanor?

APPLY ICE

<u>Meals</u>

- This is an easy way to remember which is your drink and your bread plate. With your left hand, use your thumb, pointer finger, and middle finger to form a "b," which represents bread. On your right hand, form a "d" with your thumb, pointer finger, and middle finger, which represents drink. This little trick can eliminate embarrassment when trying to decide which is your drink or bread plate.
- Another trick to remember when deciding which is your bread plate and drink is this: BMW stands for Bread, Meal, and Water. Remembering this analogy reminds you that your bread is on your left, the meal is in the middle, and your water (or other drinks) is on the right.
- Take a picture of formal and casual table settings so the next time you go out for a nice meal you have an easy reminder to be seen before sitting down at the table.
- If all else fails and you don't know which utensils or plates to use, watch your host or hostess and take your cues from them.

- If in doubt, when setting a table for a party, keep a picture on your phone of a table setting guide for a formal and casual dinner party.

<u>Office</u>

- Appoint someone in your office to make rounds periodically throughout the day to make sure junk or trash hasn't accumulated in the office or waiting areas.
- Appoint someone in your office to touch up furniture that has been scratched or dented once a month.
- Periodically have an outsider comment on the smell in the office. Is it pleasant, offensive, or neutral? Remember, you want to attach a pleasant smell to your meetings or appointments so people will think fondly of their time with you.
- Strategically place mirrors around the office so that, when saying goodbye to clients, you can take a glance to make sure you are buttoned, zipped, and tucked appropriately to leave a great last impression.
- Practice your exiting conversation verbiage for different types of clients to make an appropriate goodbye.
- Have a gift closet stocked with different items, ribbons, and paper so that when the need arises, you have an appropriate gift and don't panic while leaving a great impression on a potential client.

- Make it a habit to turn off your cell phone and watch before a client meeting or speaking engagement.

Manners, also commonly referred to as etiquette, are so much more than just setting a nice table for dinner. Even if you are dealing with people who have never been trained in etiquette or manners, you are subconsciously communicating to others that you are showing respect and creating a non-threatening atmosphere so you can earn the trust of potential clients, model polite behavior for colleagues, and keep positive, warm relationships with friends.

Using manners is about showing courtesy toward clients, patients, friends, colleagues, and strangers just about everywhere you go. You never know who is watching or with whom you will conduct business. People like to do business with those they can trust and appreciate, and manners provide a vehicle to do just that. Learning manners is like learning the difference between experiencing a five-star hotel versus an economy motel. You have educated yourself and know the different types of hotels, which puts you in a position to talk to anyone about hotels of different calibers. If you only knew about the economy motel, you would have trouble relating to or earning business from someone with five-star hotel experience.

By educating yourself about manners, you will equip yourself with the tools you need to deal with all kinds of people and calm the subconscious fears of those around you. You'll be able to earn trust, create a positive office atmosphere, retain clients or patients, and maintain great relationships with friends and family. Remember this three-step method of ICE and use it at all times.

Manners have changed through the years, due to things like a worldwide pandemic, cell phones, social media, and shifting cultural norms. The idea is to continue polite behavior, think about others (even if you don't know how to handle a situation), be aware of involving others in conversation, think about your demeanor and appearance, and reduce fear.

ICE—Impressions, Communication, and Empathy—is an easy three-step method to help you remember how to turn your manners into money. Just remember, it pays to mind your manners!

ABOUT THE AUTHOR

Robin Marriott is the Founder and CEO of Manners Mean Money. In the early 2000s, Robin saw the need for CEOs, business owners, executives, and individuals to become aware of and updated on the importance of manners to experience the positive effects they bring. Robin has several degrees, licenses, certifications, careers, and life experiences, which she has combined to offer businesses and individuals strategies for financial improvement. She has been a university educator, keynote speaker, physician coach, business etiquette liaison, and business owner. She has worked with people from a variety of financial and educational backgrounds. Robin leverages her extensive education and experience to strategize methods to increase ROI, earn client trust, and create a positive work environment. She has been married to her husband, Dr. Ronny Marriott, for thirty-seven years. They have collaborated on three books and have three grown children: Molly, Morgan, and Ryan.

NOTES

EPIGRAPH

1. Paul J. Zak, *Trust Factor: The Science of Creating High-Performance Companies* (New York: AMACOM, 2017), 129.

1. TURNING MANNER$ INTO MONEY

1. "Amygdala," Cleveland Clinic, last reviewed by Cleveland Clinic medical professional on April 11, 2023, https://my.clevelandclinic.org/health/body/24894-amygdala.

2. IMPRESSIONS

1. Serenity Gibbons, "You And Your Business Have 7 Seconds To Make A First Impression: Here's How To Succeed," Forbes, June 19, 2018, https://www.forbes.com/sites/serenitygibbons/2018/06/19/you-have-7-seconds-to-make-a-first-impression-heres-how-to-succeed/.
2. Jon Michail, "Strong Nonverbal Skills Matter Now More than Ever in this 'New Normal,'" Forbes, August 24, 2020, https://www.forbes.com/sites/forbescoachescouncil/2020/08/24/strong-nonverbal-skills-matter-now-more-than-ever-in-this-new-normal/?sh=2ce95c295c61.
3. Roger Kreuz and Richard Roberts, "Proxemics 101: Understanding Personal Space Across Cultures," The MIT Press Reader, posted December 22, 2019, https://thereader.mitpress.mit.edu/understanding-personal-space-proxemics/ .
4. "Personal Space by Country 2024," World Population Review, https://worldpopulationreview.com/country-rankings/personal-space-by-country.
5. "Personal Space by Country 2024," World Population Review, https://worldpopulationreview.com/country-rankings/personal-space-by-country.
6. Gabriel Cruz, "100 Funny Quotes About Smelling Good that will Laugh Your Way to Freshness," March 31, 2023, https://letslearnslang.com/funny-quotes-about-smelling-good/.
7. Marisa Sanfilippo, "The Smells that Make Shoppers Spend More," Business News Daily, January 24, 2024, https://www.businessnewsdaily.com/3469-smells-shoppers-spend-more.html.
8. Waio, "The Power of Smell as a Tool in the Marketing Strategy," Brand Minds, April 26, 2017, https://brandminds.com/the-power-of-

smell-as-a-tool-in-the-marketing-strategy/.

9. Chelsea Stone, "8 Smells that Can Make You Happier," The Healthy, September 29, 2017,
https://www.thehealthy.com/mental-health/happiness/happy-smells/.
10. Tony Robbins, "Improve Your Tone of Voice in Communication," TonyRobbins.com, accessed February 10, 2024, https://www.tonyrobbins.com/love-relationships/watching-your-tone/.
11. Ben C. Fletcher, D.Phil., "What Your Clothes Might Be Saying About You," Psychology Today, April 20, 2013, https://www.psychologytoday.com/us/blog/do-something-different/201304/what-your-clothes-might-be-saying-about-you.
12. Zachary Mach, "Wearing This Color Makes You Instantly Less Attractive, Research Shows," Best Life, September 15, 2020, https://bestlifeonline.com/worst-color-attractive/.

3. COMMUNICATION

1. Richard P. Console, Jr., "Bad Bedside Manner or Medical Malpractice?," The National Law Review, March 25, 2021, https://www.natlawreview.com/article/bad-bedside-manner-or-medical-malpractice.
2. Silvia Pencak, "Top 50+ Social Media Quotes," PLC, accessed February 10, 2024, https://silviapencak.com/top-50-social-media-quotes/.
3. Silvia Pencak, "Top 50+ Social Media Quotes," PLC, accessed February 10, 2024, https://silviapencak.com/top-50-social-media-quotes/.
4. Cell Phone Quotes, Brainy Quote, accessed February 10, 2024, https://www.brainyquote.com/topics/cell-phone-quotes.
5. Sarah Kay Bierle, "Lincoln Writes a Thank You Note," Emerging Civil War, December 26, 2015, https://emergingcivilwar.com/2015/12/26/lincoln-writes-a-thank-you-note/.

4. EMPATHY

1. Miss Manners, "Miss Manners: Avoid Provocative Knife Placement During Thanksgiving," *The Washington Post*, November 20, 2011, https://www.washingtonpost.com/lifestyle/style/miss-manners-avoid-provocative-knife-placement-during-thanksgiving/2011/11/03/gIQAaQKJcN_story.html.